BEFORE THE FIRE DOGS STEAL THE SUN

Next Wave: New Directions in Women's Studies

A SERIES EDITED BY

INDERPAL GREWAL, CAREN KAPLAN, AND ROBYN WIEGMAN

BEFORE THE FIRE DOGS STEAL THE SUN

AN ELEGY

Crystal Mun-hye Baik

DUKE UNIVERSITY PRESS   DURHAM AND LONDON   2026

© 2026 DUKE UNIVERSITY PRESS
This work is licensed under a Creative Commons
Attribution-NonCommercial-NoDerivatives
4.0 International License, available at https://
creativecommons.org/licenses/by-nc-nd/4.0/.
Project Editor: Lisa Lawley
Designed by Matthew Tauch
Typeset in Warnock Pro and Comma Base
by Copperline Book Services

Library of Congress Cataloging-in-Publication Data
Names: Baik, Crystal Mun-hye author
Title: Before the fire dogs steal the sun : an elegy / Crystal
Mun-hye Baik.
Other titles: Next wave (Duke University Press)
Description: Durham : Duke University Press, 2026. | Series:
Next wave: new directions in women's studies | Includes
bibliographical references and index.
Identifiers: LCCN 2025035456 (print)
LCCN 2025035457 (ebook)
ISBN 9781478038641 paperback
ISBN 9781478033769 hardcover
ISBN 9781478062257 ebook
ISBN 9781478094609 ebook/other
Subjects: LCSH: Baik, Crystal Mun-hye | Collective
memory—Korea | Grief | Korean War, 1950–1953—Social
aspects | Korean Americans—Biography | Koreans—
United States | Korean diaspora
Classification: LCC DS916.55 .B35 2026 (print) |
LCC DS916.55 (ebook) | DDC 951.904/2092—dc23/eng/20251117
LC record available at https://lccn.loc.gov/2025035456
LC ebook record available at https://lccn.loc.gov/2025035457

Cover art: Sun Young Kang, *neither here nor there*, 2017.
Courtesy of the artist.

THIS BOOK IS FREELY AVAILABLE IN AN OPEN ACCESS
EDITION THANKS TO THE GENEROUS SUPPORT OF THE
UNIVERSITY OF CALIFORNIA LIBRARIES.

For those who have persisted.

For those who have returned.

                Young Ok Baik

                Inki Baik

                Sukyoon Kim

                Yong Soon Min

                Palestine

A CIRCLE OF STORIES

NOTE TO READERS ix

An End Is a Return to the Beginning 1

The Eye of the Storm 13

I. 아버지 ‖ FATHER · A Cooking Lesson 67

II. 어머니 ‖ MOTHER

The Wind Phone 45

The Diasporic Family Album 98

III. THE MEMORY KEEPER · Grief and Return 117

Posthumous Translation 147

IV. INVOCATION · A Protection Spell Cristiana Kyung-hye Baik 159

ACKNOWLEDGMENTS 163 · NOTES 169

BIBLIOGRAPHY 177 · INDEX 183 · CREDITS 187

NOTE TO READERS

Korean words in this book are translated into English using the McCune–Reischauer and Revised Romanization systems. An exception is the spelling of family names; I have chosen to maintain the original spelling used by my parents and family in the United States. In some cases, Korean names are spelled the ways that they are written in East Asian contexts: surname followed by first name. I have made exceptions for writers, artists, scholars, and family who consistently use their first names followed by surnames. Last, I have chosen to decapitalize the *north* and *south* in "North Korea" and "South Korea," given that these are fictional designations forged through the destructive violence of colonial occupation and empire.

AN END IS A RETURN TO THE BEGINNING.

ON DECEMBER 2, 2022, my mother experienced what one therapist described as a "break from reality" and was institutionalized at a psychiatric facility. During her emergency stay, my father drove his Toyota Camry to a nearby park, overturning it in the process. Two days later, he died in my parents' home. When my mother was later released to the care of her three daughters, she came back home a transformed person, someone we hardly recognized.

In a span of one week, my parents as I knew them disappeared.

....

In the immediate weeks that followed, I was immobilized by relentless waves of panic and despair. Following Mom and Dad's retirement from their convenience store, I imagined that their days would be filled with more ease—even if illness would be an inevitable part of their lives. For the last decade of his life, my father navigated the debilitating conditions of diabetes and end-stage renal disease, while my mother struggled with chronic depression. But I could never have anticipated what happened to my parents that winter. The circumstances surrounding my father's death were also murky. He was nearly blind and had not driven a car in over three years. Even now, I am uncertain whether his car crash was intentional. But as distraught as I felt, my grief did not seem wholly cut off from my everyday emotions. Rather, it seemed to be an unwieldy outgrowth of an anguish I had long harbored about my parents' precarious lives in the United States, and the specter of family secrets that hovered, like white noise, just above the semblance of normalcy.

The unsettling sense that my grief was not new but gnarled in something older intensified as I attempted to find my father's estranged family in Korea and learn more about my mother's depressive episodes. Over meals, in phone conversations, and in email correspondence, I spoke with several of my mother's siblings about their family history in Korea. Though our conversations were often filled with pauses, an auntie and two uncles patiently answered my questions the best that they could. I also spent time with family photographs I inherited from Uncle Sukyoon, my mother's 남동생 (namtongsaeng), or baby brother. Given my father's total severance from his family, locating his history was a more haphazard process. Besides a handful of photographs and a fuzzy video recording of a family funeral, the only other entry points into my father's history were a few anecdotes shared by my parents, and published writing about and by Baik Cheol, my paternal grandfather, who was a prominent—and controversial—literary scholar in south Korea until his death in 1985.

As I assembled a makeshift archive consisting of correspondence, family recipes, translated texts, photographs, dreams, rumors, and mourning rituals, glimmers of a diasporic family history materialized. Remnants of story cohered around war, abandonment, and family separation, as well as profound sorrow and colonial complicity. Gathering these disparate stories intimated that my father's death and mother's hospitalization were embedded in larger stories that did not begin or end with them. Though not inevitable, these events were points within historical trajectories catapulted by decades of war, upheaval, and migration. Situated in this way, the calamities of 2022 were long in the making, even before my birth and the births of my sisters. Without my knowing it, my grief became a portal into feeling and writing about Korean diasporic genealogies of war in relation to, but also beyond, my family of origin.

....

Before the Fire Dogs Steal the Sun: An Elegy is conceived from this raw space of grief and mourning. It crystallizes through an emotionally driven or a felt form of writing I describe as *diasporic grief*. My understanding of diasporic grief is grounded in my training as a feminist scholar, writer, and memory keeper. In particular, I am grateful for the expansive work of Black, Indigenous, and women of color writers like Audre Lorde and Dian Million who have taught me how crucial it is to theorize with and write through emotions.[1] In essays like "The Uses of Anger" and "Poetry Is Not a Luxury," Lorde rejects Cartesian logics that sever the mind from one's body, senses, and feelings. On the contrary, knowledge, for Lorde, is intimately entwined with the body and feelings, which provide an "incredible reserve of creativity and power."[2] In her scholarship, Million (Tanana Athabascan) centers the firsthand testimonials of First Nations women living in the settler state of Canada. As political acts of dissidence, these harrowing narratives of racial and sexual violence not only refuse the measured objectivity of the white settler gaze; rather, as emotionally inflected knowledge, the constellation of words encompassed by these testimonials also constitutes *felt theory* and fundamentally shifts what can be uttered about the brutal violence experienced by Native women in Turtle Island.

Building on these feminist offerings, diasporic grief as an embodied form of writing is tied to the uncanny sense that my sorrow was not only a visceral response to what befell my parents. Rather, the unfurling of my grief moved me to articulate an interlacing of historical conditions that impacted the becoming of my parents, and the complicated ways I loved and lost them. Putting into words what I had been hesitant to verbalize, or thoughts I did not even know I needed to articulate, catalyzed reparative ways of thinking and writing about my parents and their militarized histories.

When I started to write again following my father's death and mother's hospitalization, my intention was not to write another book. I instead wanted to provide shelter for the torrent of questions that were difficult, even shameful, to ask out loud. These spurts of writing became a haven for disclosure. But as sentences filled the computer screen, I was taken aback by the frenetic velocity with which I wrote. In the first several days, I typed nearly thirty pages of single-spaced text. There was a cathartic freedom to my thinking and writing I had not experienced in a long while, especially as someone trained in academe. This openness was conditioned by an understanding that I was not writing to "intervene" in a body of literature or to craft an "argument," at least in the most conventional sense. I took to writing because it was the only thing that seemed to loosen the density of grief lodged in my body. Mourning through the quietude of writing allowed me to acknowledge all that I did not know, while spending time with my parents in more patient ways. Writing *with* rather than *against* my grief created elegiac space for the tears, anger, and contradictions that filtered into the stories I gathered about my family. While I remained in this grievous place, it was impossible to write about my parents' lives without addressing the unstable parts of their upbringing and their migration from Korea to the United States in 1984. In turn, this transoceanic migration was a single moment within diasporic histories that transpired through colonial occupation, war, poverty, and peninsular division.

Diasporic grief in the context of Korea holds specific meaning and weight. When I write about who and what has been lost, I am not only in communion with the dead. My mourning extends to the living whose pasts collapse with their present and future. I lament for the disappeared whose fates remain unknown. I grieve for the partitioned land marred by subterranean mines and disappeared bodies. Diasporic grief unhinges the boundaries that separate the living from the dead, the human from the nonhuman.

Between 1950 and 1953, up to ten million people in Korea were separated from their loved ones by a border imposed by colonial forces that slashed the peninsula along its belly. This fortified line remains today, and most separated families, at least those who are alive, wait in numbed agony with little to no information about missing family and friends. Like so many other Koreans I know, my family was ripped apart and reconstructed by division. My paternal grandfather and maternal grandparents were born in the provinces of North P'yŏng'an and South Hamgyŏng in northern Korea. To the best of my knowledge, my mother's and father's parents left their homes in the north for Seoul and Beijing, respectively, between 1946 and 1950. They were never able to return. What they left behind were families, friends, land, rivers, and so many other things I cannot name. My grief partially stems from the realization that the geopolitical conditions that led to my family's banishment from their ancestral homes remain firmly in place today. Currently, as someone who carries a US passport, I am barred from visiting what is now north Korea, a country that has been bombed, incessantly ridiculed, and demonized by the United States.[3] While I will never definitively know the full extent to which war and division transformed the lives of my family, this book compelled me to revisit childhood scenes of violence, addiction, and refusal as plausible sites of militarized rupture that have never been fully reckoned with.

Through grief, my writing became a bridge that opened me to my parents' suppressed memories, even if through speculative terms. There is so much I didn't know about my parents and their childhoods in Korea, and this remains true today. But rather than an emotional affliction, my diasporic grief became a tender way to return to my parents and the absences they left. Locating my mother, father, and myself within these braided ancestral histories expanded how I came to understand familial lineage, in relation to not only kinship but also land, water, and place; food and embodied memories; language, both alive and lost; and Korean feminist comrades, both living and deceased. Familial genealogy is a *multitude* rather than a single naturalized thread. How we hold, feel, and name family is not just through biology, nor is it solely through the web of social affinities we nurture beyond blood ties. It is an interweaving of both, with people forging varied permutations depending on where and how they are located, and the social norms that dictate who can be loved and who must be banished. But in writing this book, it was important for me to spend time with my mother's and father's kinship ties to acknowledge that their families, as refugees, did not have the option to stay together. Although our families of origin can enact extraordinary harm, they can also be imperfect places of care that are torn asunder by war, dispossession, and militarized colonial destruction. Families of origin thus are not naturally intact or given forms that should be taken for granted. They are, instead, shifting formations defined by power. In this way, diasporic grief does not encompass only bereavement and sorrow. It is porous and generative, enveloping the ways we care for and keep memory, and our capacity to feel and name contentious lineages through thinking, writing, and ritual.[4]

By drawing on diasporic grief as a felt practice of writing, I vehemently reject the distance expected between scholarship and the richness of emotional life. Too often academics treat these as oppositional poles that should or can never touch. In contrast to this assumption, this book centers personal forms of address, feelings and sensations, and everyday moments like the cooking of meals and solitary walks. An emphasis on the mundane dimensions of daily life provides readers with the opportunity to slow down and consider the complex personhoods of those subjected to the violence of war and occupation. My decision to attend to these routinized moments is intentional, given that colonized peoples are rarely afforded the opportunity to exist—in life or on paper—as fully fleshed beings who love, hate, eat, rest, and desire. By refusing to abide by the elisions produced by institutional and familial violence, my writing engages diasporic histories through a speculative archive of letters, extended conversations with the dead, and deferred encounters with family photographs. As Christina Sharpe and Brandon Shimoda teach us through their poetic writing, critical uses of our imagination are crucial if we are to survive the insidious erasures of history and memory—which are never accidental or innocuous.[5] Rather, they are conditioned by vectors of power, like white supremacy, heteropatriarchy, and class violence, that mirror back to us the societal values that dictate who can be known and commemorated, and who must be vanquished from memory.

As an *intimate* cultural history that refracts the militarized colonial histories of Korea through the lens of the "I," this book places at front and center several questions that guided me as I grieved without knowing where my writing would take me. What ethical stakes and vulnerabilities arise when scholars are implicated in the histories of violence we study and write about?[6] How do we write our diasporic family histories when they can only be encountered through silence, insinuation, translation, and estrangement? What vocabulary must we conjure to describe the intimate scale of harm induced by war, even if such forms of expression evade the institutionalized language of academe? Last, I consider the sobering questions offered by Sora Y. Han in *Mu, 49 Marks of Abolition*. All this time, "Who have I been writing to? Who have I been writing for?"[7]

....

Although this book is written in a personal voice, it does not offer a comprehensive or definitive biography. While this was never a goal of this project, offering a "complete" family history, no matter how much we *think* we know, is an impossible task for different reasons.

For one, memory is a selective enterprise. In my parents' families, it is the eldest patriarchs who are remembered, with their professional and prolific accomplishments as intellectuals and healers well documented in family mythology and institutional archives. In contrast, the women in my family, including both of my grandmothers, exist as spotty traces in the family memory archive. While I know relatively little about my grandmothers' lives, I know that they ultimately married older men and were raised to believe that their primary roles in life were to be self-sacrificing wives and caregivers. A rigorous contention with gender norms and social expectations thus is crucial to *what* and *how* I write: While these gaps in family knowledge were challenging to navigate, the juxtaposition of gendered familial presences and absences enabled subversive routes to touch memory. Drawing from my paternal grandfather's professional writing, accolades, and intellectual records, I imagine the sticky underlining of unspoken intimacies affixed to these public recollections. For my maternal grandmother, I consider the socioeconomic and gendered strictures that limited resources and opportunities available to her; at the same time, I refuse her wholesale erasure by dreaming onto paper the submerged possibilities that could have been.

For reasons I do not fully disclose in this book, I do not extensively write about my maternal grandfather and paternal grandmother, though momentary encounters with them percolate throughout these pages.

In lieu of completeness, diasporic grief prompts social imaginaries and reparative ways to dwell, think, and write with what we don't know. Silences, innuendos, and hesitations are not workarounds in my writing. They are its conditions of possibility. They give me permission to summon stories occluded from the historical record *and* the family memory archive through speculative forms of writing. Different genres of writing that range from the epistolary to spellcasting modes potentiate lines of open-ended exploration foreclosed by more traditional methods of academic writing and research. Feeling and writing in improvised ways was not only a liberating experience; it was necessary for this book.

With this in mind, this book unfolds through four parts: "아버지 || Father," "어머니 || Mother," "The Memory Keeper," and "Invocation." These sections are enmeshed with overlapping questions and responses that return throughout the book. The first three parts each encompass two chapters, the first written in narrative prose and the second in a different mode of writing that spans from letter writing to the visual essay to the grief ritual. The fourth and last part of this book is a protection spell composed by the poet Cristiana Kyung-hye Baik, a longtime collaborator, a confidante, and my twin sister.

Before the Fire Dogs Steal the Sun attends to what is possible and what we may need to let go of when we dive into the ocean that is our diasporic histories. In the past several years, I have learned that the depth of these waters, beneath tumultuous waves, is vast if not infinite.

....

I leave my generous readers with two last notes. First, even as I draw on Korean cosmologies of ancestral mourning and grief in my writing to consider the impact of unresolved violence within my diasporic family, I do so without using the cultural paradigm of 한, or han. *Han* refers to a collective sadness embodied by the Korean people as an ethnic community, due to generations of sedimented trauma resulting from empire, war, sexual violence, and family separation.[8] While I find this term powerful and impactful in how it addresses violence as complicatedly layered, I worry that its overgeneralized use in public discourse has diluted the specificities of historical violence. To a certain degree, han in the social imaginary has become an umbrella term that captures a blended multitude of traumas, like sexual violence, colonial displacement, and financial ruin, sustained across generations of Koreans.

Consequently, these generalized articulations have stymied the development of a critical vocabulary that challenges racist, sexist, and ableist assumptions in Korea and the Korean diaspora. While unintentional, diagnosing an emotional condition for an entire people, regardless of time, circumstance, and location, can pigeonhole women's bodies for the patriotic project of nation building. This is especially true in discussions that tackle "taboo" and effeminized disabilities like chronic depression, suicidal ideation, and madness, all matters taken up in this book. For example, as the devastating histories of Korean "comfort women"—who endured years of rape, assault, and sexual slavery under the Japanese colonial regime—have taught us, women are too often perceived as the embodiment of colonial harm and shame in Korea and an impediment to national progress. When it comes to Korean "comfort women," han has been taken up precisely in this manner by conservative pundits, politicians, and governing administrations alike. These actors identify Japanese colonialism as the main culprit of national trauma in Korea, even while they simultaneously treat "comfort women" as a contentious issue that could disrupt bilateral relations with Japan.[9] As a result, heteropatriarchal, ableist, and racist norms that directly contribute to gender and sexual violence remain intact. This book conjures an alternative language to name submerged forms of violence that chronically manifest, without relying on untroubled notions of *inherited* trauma. That is, rather than diagnosing depression, psychic pain, and grief as naturalized inheritances transmitted from generation to generation, I describe the systemic conditions that reproduce destructive forms of violence in localized ways.

Finally, the title of this book draws inspiration from a line included in the chapter "The Wind Phone." It alludes to the Korean mythology of the 불개 (bulgae), or fire dogs, which narrates the origins of solar and lunar eclipses. In this ancient myth, the kingdom of darkness releases its ferocious bulgae to chase and capture the sun and moon. In essence, eclipses are the evidential work of the bulgae, as they leave gaping bite marks in these luminescent bodies. These events are thought to unleash intensified spiritual energies, while exposing the underbelly of the world. At the same time, an alternative universe is created, where time stands still, even expands. In this temporal break, the living can encounter the dead with care and caution. As they return across space and time, the bulgae and their bite marks are cosmic reminders of the shape-shifting nature of celestial bodies as they dissolve from solid spheres to glowing crescents to a hidden presence. Inevitably, these passages of violence and disappearance are entangled with transformation, even possibility. This book is conceived with this myth in mind. When my world was collapsing and closing in on me, my writing provided a co-cooned sanctuary where time stretched long enough for me to be quiet and still. In this soft space of reprieve, I breathed through the changing seasons as I mourned for my parents and ancestors. At this moment of planetary catastrophe, where there seems to be less and less time, I am grateful to have had this opportunity to return and remain through the gifts of listening and writing.

아버지 ‖ FATHER

THE EYE OF THE STORM

Dad drove his car on a warm, bone-dry Saturday.

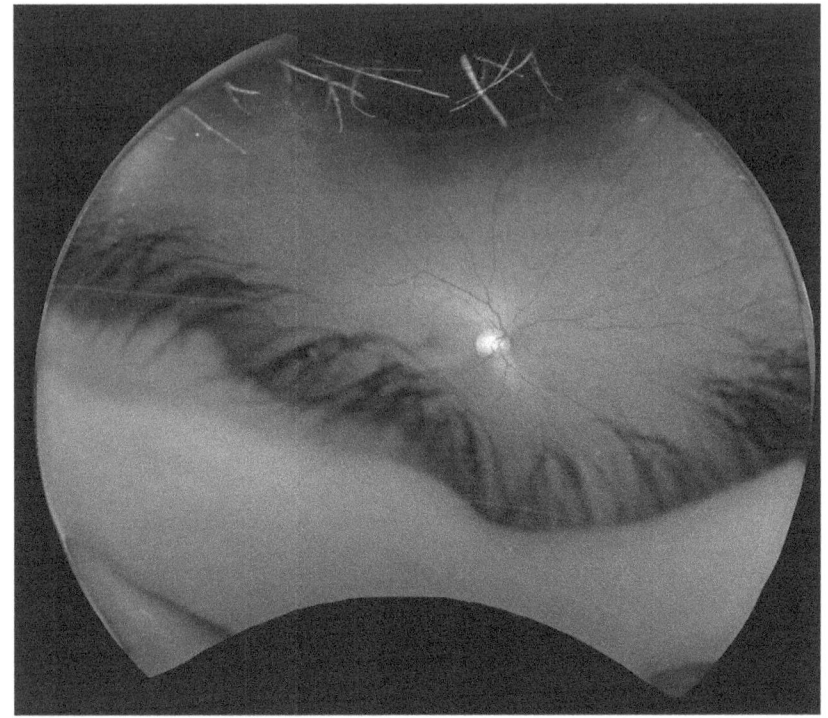

He died the following Monday.

ON A RAINY DAY, I arrive at my optometrist's office for my annual checkup. During the appointment, I am provided with an optomap, or a high-resolution retinal image used to gauge the health of a patient's eyes. But this technical description does not capture how otherworldly these images are. Awash with a soft, glowing green, these eye portraits remind me of NASA photographs of the solar system, replete with the optic disc—a luminescent sun orb floating in the center of the photograph—with delicate branches of blood vessels jutting from its yellow belly. When I look at these photographs, I delight at the idea that there is an undetectable universe inside of me, so full of unknowns and possibilities. I am also reminded of how complicated the eye is, and how little I know the inner mechanics of my own body.

I speak with my optometrist and share concerns my identical twin sister, Cristiana—or Cris, as I call her—relayed to me regarding her eye exam months earlier. She was informed that the enlarged size of the optic nerve cupping hinted at the possibility of glaucoma. But Dr. K isn't very concerned. What could be flagged as a risk for others, she says, is likely an indicator of genetics for me. These so-called nonnormative shapes say more about the genes my parents gifted me than they do about a disease lurking in the shadows. When I hear this, I am baffled. There is so much I didn't know and understand about my father. Yet his genes partially determine how I navigate this world through my (his) eyesight.

....

In the last three years of his life, my father's eyesight deteriorated to the point where he completely lost sight in his left eye while retaining minuscule functioning in his right. Early during the COVID-19 pandemic, I would observe Dad holding a book so close to his face that his nose intermittently caressed the page. Though he never said anything to me, I sensed that his struggle to read hit him hard. Despite working sixteen-hour shifts for most of his life in the United States—first at a furniture store in Los Angeles's Koreatown, then at a gas station in El Segundo near the airport, and finally at Sunshine Market, a convenience store in the Inland Empire that he comanaged with my mother—Dad was a committed reader. Reading was one of the few activities that proved accessible and affordable. During quiet stretches at work, Dad could be found behind the bulletproof window at the store, immersed in a Korean-language newspaper or a historical novel. After my parents retired from Sunshine Market, his favorite pastime was reading in their backyard with their beloved Maltipoo, Shelly, nestled in his lap. Before I entered graduate school, Dad told me how much he relished the idea that his three daughters were avid readers. He felt that this was a common thread that meaningfully connected him to his children. When I was first hired as an assistant professor at the University of California, Riverside, I took my parents to campus during the summer of 2014. On entering my office, my father sighed as he marveled at the tall bookcases that lined the white walls, as if he was entering a cathedral of books. He walked toward the shelves, gently patting the books' spines like they were an extension of my back.

After I published my first book, *Reencounters: On the Korean War and Diasporic Memory Critique*, in 2019, my parents never asked about its subject matter. But I shared with them that my writing was influenced by their experiences as the immediate generation that grew up in the long shadow of the unended Korean War. I don't remember what their response was to this. Most likely an *Oh, I see*, or a silent nod substituting for words they couldn't say out loud. Nevertheless, my parents propped a hard copy of the book against a photograph stand near their home entryway like a prized portrait. The book is still the first object I see when I enter my parents' house.

While Cris and I worried that we had inherited glaucoma from our father, this wasn't the source of his eyesight loss. I later learned that his diabetic retinopathy resulted from the uncontrolled intake of sugar and, more precisely, the uncontrolled intake of alcohol. At some point during his youth, my father developed an addictive affinity for alcohol, with soju, red wine, and Chivas Regal being his drinks of choice. There were weeks when he would consume several bottles of wine or hard liquor every night. He didn't stop drinking until he was in his sixties, when he developed end-stage renal disease. His kidneys could no longer eliminate the toxins that had accumulated and were now swimming in his body.

Throughout my life, I have many times atomized Dad's dependence on alcohol as an individual weakness. But I know that the origins of my father's addiction are complicated, with social and cultural roots. As with many Koreans I know, drinking formed a cornerstone of Dad's personal and professional life. From the little that Mom shared with me about Dad's family, his mother and siblings drank frequently. Dad's longer-lasting friendships were cemented through a shared fondness for drinking, first at bars during college and then at work functions in Los Angeles and Orange County. As in other Korean families I grew up with, no one in my household ever spoke about therapy, nor did Dad have time to take up leisurely hobbies. When his work schedule was more flexible, Dad swam laps in the pool at our childhood home. For my father, drinking was the thing that soothed his mounting anxiety after our family moved to Fountain Valley, a sleepy suburb in Southern California, from Seoul in 1984. After this transoceanic migration, his social life was confined to my mother's family and business friends who lived in the greater Los Angeles area.

Since most of Dad's life in the United States orbited around the routinized drudgery of work, I sensed that his drinking was also a means to an end: to activate an enlivened sense of self. Though they rarely complained, my parents worked for decades in tedious jobs that offered little in return. At Sunshine Market, they spent countless hours standing behind the cramped checkout counter without breaks for meals. During our weekend visits to the store, my husband, Dan, and I would arrive to Dad napping on a thin blanket on the concrete floor behind the counter while Mom took care of customers. For fifteen years, Dad arrived at work every day at 8:00 a.m. and left for home after he closed the business just after midnight, while Mom opened the store at 6:00 a.m. and left for home by 8:00 p.m. This cycle repeated until my parents sold their business and retired in 2014. Mom later shared with me that Dad and she remained haunted by those years of exhausting labor. It's as if their embodied memories of that time calcified into a permanent layer of weathered skin that could not be softened. Following his transition to dialysis three days a week in 2014, my dad once whispered to me in Korean, *I wish I could drink again.*

But sometimes, I wonder if acknowledging these complexities is a convenient way for me to isolate the parts of Dad I hated, or to alleviate the blow of the collateral damage his drinking inflicted on our family. Mom, especially, bore the brunt of a ravenous addiction that was impossible to satiate. She worked alongside my father while raising three daughters as if she was a single parent. Amid this, she struggled to keep her depression at bay against a domestic life punctuated by financial precarity, social isolation, and explosive fights. Toward the end of Dad's life, my parents' relationship softened and became more tender, partly due to their retirement, and also because my father no longer drank. But the accrued exhaustion resulting from a turbulent marriage and the decade of care that followed Dad's kidney diagnosis—hospital visits, the management of medication, the monotonized schedule of cooking and

cleaning—hollowed my mother until she became a frail version of herself unable to decipher her own needs.

My parents' fighting was especially intense during my elementary and junior high school years. During the workweek, Dad would stagger home following a night of heavy drinking, while Mom waited alone downstairs in the dimly lit dining room. Cris and I would be wide awake, vigilantly huddled underneath the pink canopy of a flower-patterned comforter in our shared room. As we anticipated Dad's return in the darkness, we collectively held our breaths. *The calm before the storm.* At one or two in the morning, we would hear Dad's jangling key just outside the front door. Within a minute, my older sister, Coleen, would sprint down the stairs to act as a human buffer between my parents as they screamed at and lunged toward each other. When I remember the mediator role Coleen was forced to play at this young age, I mourn for the teenage version of my sister who never had the opportunity to be a carefree child. One time after he returned home from a bar, Dad shattered the kitchen window and promptly passed out on the couch with a bloody T-shirt wrapped around his hand. As our father peacefully slept, Coleen tiptoed into the kitchen, gingerly gathering the broken glass with a towel and burying the jagged shards underneath a fragrant lemon tree in the furthest corner of our backyard. To this day, I still can't look at a lemon tree without recalling that faint scent of citrus drifting in the blue stillness of twilight hours. I wonder whether the fragments of glass are still there, like buried treasure, in the backyard of our childhood home that was, ironically enough, on a street called La Esperanza, or "hope" in Spanish.

Now and then, my childhood returns to me, not as a linear progression, but as a disarray of scenes. These scenes take place in the La Esperanza house and are most vivid at night while I sleep, so much so that my dreams become a vespertine edge where the present envelops the past.

> *inhale*
> The burial of glass shards underneath the fragrant lemon tree
> Mom packing her daughters into the black Volvo with garbage bags
> overripe with clothes
> *exhale*
>
> *inhale*
> The gravelly tone of Dad's voice after drinking
> The foggy atmosphere of Mom's depression
> *exhale*

In the wake of my father's death, I have trouble reconciling these contradictory sides of him. On the one hand, Dad was a caring person with an enduring affinity for his daughters, reading, and injured animals. As Coleen and Cris both reminded me after he passed away, our father frequently shared how much he loved us, which was rare among the Korean dads we knew. On the other hand, there was a chasm between my father's words and actions: There was the person he desired to be and the person he was. Dad's drinking and its ramifications, from financial struggles to tense relations with my mother's family, inflicted damaging consequences that continue to reverberate in his afterlife. This incongruence is apparent in my words. As I look at the computer screen, I am surprised by the dissonance between the lyrical, almost beautiful phrases conjured by these memories and the constrictive density lodged in my throat.

> *Twilight Hours*
>
> *Fragrant lemon tree*
> *Overripe*
> *Gravelly tone*
> *Foggy atmosphere*
>
> ....

In reflecting on the sudden death of her husband of thirty-nine years in *The Year of Magical Thinking*, Joan Didion describes grief as debilitating waves that "weaken the knees and blind the eyes."[1] Meditating on the passing of her father, uncle, and mother, Edwidge Danticat writes about these profound losses with shock and somber acceptance.[2] In the months following my father's death and mother's hospitalization, my grief surfaced less as discombobulating waves of sorrow or moments of contemplation, and more as sharp jabs that dropped my stomach to my feet. Strangely enough, these moments struck me most often when I was a passenger in a car. When I started to wonder why, one of my undergraduate students shared something with me that resonated with my experience. *It feels as if I'm frozen in time while the rest of the world is moving without me.* Somehow, riding in a car echoed this paralysis and the ways that grief sliced time into parallel tracks that moved at varying speeds: My body remained fixed while the world outside my window flew by as a formless blur.

For some time, I didn't read or write. Emails were left unread, texts mostly unanswered. I took family medical leave from work. But slowly, the dense ball of grief I was holding fractured into an opening that brought me back to thinking and creating. In increments, I began to write again. When I returned to the computer screen in the quietude of my home office, I felt an urgency to write—a pull I had not felt for a long while. I was putting onto the page all the things I could not share with my sisters or mother because I did not want to burden them. But also, over time, I had collected in my head a litany of questions I wanted to ask my dad but never had the gumption to do so while he was alive. Paper became the transferal site and the memory archive for these long-held questions.

> *Did you ever want to be a father?*
> *Why did you stop speaking to your family?*
> *Why didn't you want to return to Korea? Where was home?*
> *What propelled you to make promises you couldn't keep?*

Even now, I am surprised by how little my sisters and I knew about our father. Though I vaguely knew Dad had siblings, we didn't know details because he was estranged from his family for nearly all our lives. Only in the process of completing his death certificate did we discover, from our mother, that my father was the third-youngest child in the family, with two sisters and a brother. As I discovered much later in my research, my dad also had two half siblings—a brother and a sister—from my grandfather's previous three marriages. We do not know whether any of his siblings are still alive. For the first time, we learned the name of Dad's mother, Choi Jeongsuk (née). In the hell of those five days between Dad's death and Mom's release from the psychiatric facility, my sisters and I cleaned and reorganized the house as best as we could. By then, the house was overrun by unopened bills and other mail, boxes of yellowed accounting papers from past businesses, and piles of unfolded clothes. Amid cleaning, we were unable to locate a single letter, document, or other ephemera that could provide some clue about our dad's past life in Korea.

More recently, I searched for Dad's family through other means. When we were in our mid-twenties, Cris had met a cousin in south Korea who at that time was a graduate student in literature at Seoul National University. While Cris warned me that the email address she had was likely defunct, I still wrote to this cousin with the desperate hope that I would reach someone, anyone, from Dad's family:

FROM: CRYSTAL BAIK
TO:—
DATE: FEBRUARY 26, 2023 10:05 A.M.
SUBJECT: HI 지혜—FROM 사촌동생

DEAR 지혜:

I'm your cousin, Crystal (문혜). I live in Los Angeles in the United States. Many, many years ago in 2006, you met my twin sister Cristiana (경혜) when she was visiting Seoul. I am sorry to share this, but my father, your uncle, passed away on 5 December 2022. I am sorry I couldn't share this earlier. Our father never put us in contact with his brothers or sisters, so there was no way to be in touch. I hope this email address is still active—and that there will be a way for us to meet in person. I should be traveling to Korea in the next year or so and can be in contact with you.

Sincerely,
Crystal Baik

As Cris predicted, the email bounced back with no forwarding contact information.

I'm uncertain why I never asked my father about his life in Korea. Despite our difficult relationship, Dad and I settled for some semblance of peace in our interactions during the last decade of his life, even if wholesale repair would never be possible. In part, my anger remained silent because I didn't know how to broach a past I preferred to forget. Dad's growing frailty also brought mortality into our consciousness, making him more dependent on my mother and me for what he used to take for granted, like driving and eating. In turn, this softened me and made my father more cognizant of his caretakers' needs. He began to massage my mother's feet in the evenings and made spontaneous phone calls to me during the workweek, as if he was attempting to make up for the turmoil of his life. Maybe it was my father's quiet way of saying *I'm sorry* without ever uttering those words. *Mun-hye-ya, it's Dad. I'm just calling because I was lonely and I wanted to let you know how much I love you, my youngest one.*

I still have not listened to his last voicemail message to me.

Relatedly, the barrier created by language made it difficult to have longer conversations with my father; Dad struggled with his English, and speaking in my conversational Korean about hairy topics is tricky. But more important, by the time I was old enough to have serious conversations with him, I intuitively sensed that I shouldn't ask him questions about his past. Dad had so thoroughly severed himself from his family that this dissociation seemed intentional. Our relationship was symbiotic in that sense. I rarely asked questions; he rarely volunteered information.

The information I've managed to pull together about my father's family has emerged from correspondence with writers and scholars about 백철, or Baik Cheol (given name Baik Se-cheol, pen name Baik Cheol), a prominent scholar and literary critic in south Korea who was my dad's father. In the past year alone, I've amassed a small library of bilingual academic and biographical texts about Baik Cheol.[3] I am able to search for these articles because I myself am a scholar with access to online databases and academic search engines. But also: Baik Cheol's status as a public figure—and more precisely, a public *male* figure who was able to pursue an intellectual profession—has generated a trove of records, like academic Wikipedia profiles and online essays, that is accessible to nearly anyone. The existence of these records has provided a way for me to write about his and my father's lives with some sense of footing. This, of course, is not the case for others in my paternal family, including my grandmother, Choi Jeong-

suk, who remains a mystery to me. From email correspondence with colleagues in south Korea, I know that Jeongsuk was my grandfather's fourth and last wife, that she was seventeen years his junior, and that she came from a humble family in Suwŏn. But this assortment of details is what I have to conjure her into corporeal form. When I mention this to my mother and inquire about Grandma's life, she pauses before telling me that I should stop asking questions about "that cruel woman."

But who should I ask?, I mutter to myself. There is no one left to speak with in our family.

Recently, a scholar who teaches in south Korea emailed me a sympathetic note to express how bewildering it must be to learn the most elemental details of my paternal family—the names of my father's siblings, for instance—from strangers in the academic world. In my response to them, I share that I feel fortunate. Given my father's estrangement from his family, I am grateful that these buried connections surfaced in the first place. I only spent time with my paternal grandparents as a baby, so my memories of them are always mediated through the few photographs I inherited from my parents. In my favorite image of them, my grandfather is holding me in his lap and tenderly looking down at my rosy face with a soft expression. My grandmother is seated next to him with her arms folded around Cris.

....

While the posthumous search for my father has been a frustrating experience, I have been consoled by, of all things, my work as a scholar of Korean diasporic studies and feminist memory work. In an unexpected sense, it is as if my training primed me for this exact moment.

When I first considered the litany of things I didn't know about my dad's life, it dawned on me that the frustrations I was navigating were not unique to my family. Instead, the gaping holes in my knowledge reflected a web of diasporic stories I had listened to about the Korean War in my previous research. In these firsthand testimonial narratives, many of the young people I directly spoke or corresponded with did not know the names of their more recent ancestors or had patchy knowledge of their family lineages. Others I spoke with were cut off from their birth families, birthplace, and birth tongue as babies through an adoption industry that originated in Korea during the years of US military governance between 1945 and 1948.[4] I realized then that it would be difficult to delve into the ambiguities of my father's life without at least speculating on the repercussions of war and peninsular division within my own family.

Nearly all my scholarly writing, to date, explores the complexities of the Korean War and the ways that different generations in the diaspora encounter the rippling effects of a seventy-year war that, quite literally, has yet to end.[5] But the consequences I write about are not the typical associations that may come to mind when war and militarization are discussed in mainstream media—for instance, the images and sounds of battlefields, soldiers and veterans, drones, and camptowns. Rather, I look at how the prolongation of war produces reverberations so thoroughly engrained in everyday life—from the places we move to and live in, to the languages we lose and speak, to our most intimate feelings, to the people we recognize as family—that it becomes challenging to extricate war's domino effects from the grist of our lives.[6] These insidious enmeshments, I have written, produce their own gaps, secrets, and questions, some that refuse to be answered with the precision we desire.

After my family arrived in the United States when I was four, I didn't understand why the names of my dad's family, besides his father, were never mentioned in our home. I couldn't make sense of what I, at the time, interpreted as bizarre responses from my parents. In one incident during high school, my parents became agitated when Cris and I became involved with "political activity" (something as innocuous as joining a local chapter of Amnesty International!). In another incident, my mom called me, panicked that Cris had been kidnapped by north Korean government spies when she traveled to P'yŏngyang through a diasporic educational program organized by Nodutdol, a grassroots organization based in New York City.[7] When I was growing up, our family didn't have the time or money to take vacations. Still, my parents never once voiced a longing to visit Korea together. Mom and Dad, it seemed, desired to maintain an impermeable distance between Korea and our family. By and large, their efforts were successful. As I became older, I grew more uncertain, even fearful, of what I might find in Korea. I didn't return to Seoul until I was thirty-five, and by then, my father's ties with his family were completely severed.

Only recently did I discover that both of my parents' families had originally come from northern Korea and were displaced several times during a three-decade period: first, by education policies during the Japanese colonial era (1910–45); second, by the joint United States–Soviet division of the Korean Peninsula in 1945; and, third, by large-scale armed fighting that erupted in Korea by June 1950. My maternal grandparents crossed into southern Korea in 1946 with their young children in tow (my mother had not been born yet), but most of their immediate and extended family remained in the north.[8] Though I am still learning about my father's family and have amended this writing several times as details have emerged, they likely settled in Seoul by 1950. Similarly to my mother's kin, most of Dad's family on his paternal side remained in northern Korea.

Due to the anticommunist state ideology that determined every facet of life in south Korea after 1948, being associated with north Korea in any capacity was so dangerous that people commonly expunged names from their hojŏk, or family registries. Under the military dictatorship of Pak Chŏnghŭi, the south Korean president from 1961 until his assassination in 1979, the government encouraged citizens to report "suspicious" family members to local officials. Police forces arrested those labeled as communists or political dissidents, while others suspected of having family ties to north Korea, or "red lines in the genealogical record," were banished from the workforce.[9] When my parents were coming of age in south Korea, their compulsory textbooks were filled with illustrations where Koreans in the north were portrayed as red-horned devils gleefully eating children. Since Mom and Dad both had relatives in the north, I suspect that their respective families took precautions to ensure their collective safety. These protective measures could have included significant revisions to their family registries, as well as emigration from south Korea to the United States and elsewhere. On my mother's side, everyone in her immediate family permanently moved to the greater New York City area, northern Virginia, and California by the mid-1980s.

As I speculate on the reasons that propelled my family's migrations across the finger of the peninsula and beyond, I consider how the far-reaching tentacles of war permeated my father's life, infiltrating his movements in and out of this world. Both he and my mother were born during a time when war decimated any semblance of stability. In a literal sense, their introduction to the world was through the red luminescence of napalm. What is it like to be born during a time when the world is on fire? What could have possibly happened to my father in his youth that he learned, so effectively, to keep his fears as secrets that accompanied him to the afterlife? I am reminded of what literary scholar Joo Ok Kim repeatedly inquires in the closing of her book, *Warring Genealogies: Race, Kinship, and the Korean War*: "What is our relationship to the Korean War?"[10]

I will never know the answers to these questions. But in this white expanse, other possibilities emerge. These residual gaps become the interstices through which I conjure into language what was or could have been. I want to remain in this grove of silences, these shadowed crevices between knowing and not knowing, as I grieve for my father and his family.

....

It is April 2018, and I am nearly finished writing my first book, *Reencounters*. Dan and I are at my parents' stucco home in Montclair, celebrating my father's seventieth birthday.

To mark the occasion, Dan and I bring a large tray of fresh sashimi from a sushi restaurant in Los Angeles because we know it's my father's favorite food. It is a feast: There are generous cuts of lean and fatty tuna, along with thinly sliced scallop, squid, salmon, and grilled unagi, or eel, served over small mounds of white rice. Dad is elated because these days, he is unable to drink and eat most things. Slowly, kidney disease has dwindled his meals to a bland list of permitted vegetables, fruits, nuts, some grains, and water. This past year, he has lost so much weight that he resembles a child masquerading in his father's pants and shirt. Whether it's a good decision or not, Mom and I always make an exception for Dad on his birthday and on Christmas: Twice a year, he is able to eat healthy amounts of rice, fish, and a sliver of cake for dinner. My father doesn't take these meals for granted. He delights in every bite and morsel.

While Shelly desperately paws at my mother's feet for food, my father is in a jubilant mood, laughing and happily licking his fingers.

Mun-hye-ya, you know that your grandfather loved fish too. My love for sashimi is from him.

I stop eating and look up from my plate. Dad has *never* mentioned my grandfather like this—so breezily, in passing—before.

Oh yeah? What kind of fish? I casually ask between bites of food.

Yes, he really loved this restaurant in P'yŏngyang that served fish—all kinds of fish too.

That's where your family lived, ah-ba?

For the next fifteen minutes, while Dan and Mom are listening, my father and I converse in our broken Korean-English about his family's experiences during the Korean War. I am gentle in my questioning, never asking direct questions but simply nodding my head or asking, 어디? 왜? 진짜? *Where? Why? Oh really?*

The conversation is brief, without textured details, but in that window of time, my father describes his family's displacements throughout the Korean War:

My father migrated from North P'yŏng'an Province to P'yŏngyang.

Our family fled from P'yŏngyang to Seoul in 1950,

then from Seoul to the city of Suwŏn in 1951 or 1952,

then back to Seoul in 1953.

While Dad is sharing this story with me, my mother grabs a piece of paper to scribble notes for me, including the places he names in rapid succession. Though I don't utter a single word to her, Mom knows how meaningful it is for me to hear about my father's family. She hands me the piece of paper so I can jot down my own observations. Soon Dad signals that he is ready to close the conversation. Patting his stomach and yawning as he stands up from the table, he shares in Korean, *Thank you, Mun-hye-ya and Dan. I'm full, so I'm going to step out with Shelly for a walk.* Tacitly, I understand that I shouldn't press further.

Years later when I touch this piece of paper with its dizzying marks and my misspelled words in Korean, I can still hear the decisive tone of Dad's voice inflected with nostalgia. *This is where I was from, Munhye-ya.* In our conversation, there are also memories, names, and relations that my father quietly kept to himself. But even while these remnants remain silent, they are not wholly absent or missing from what he uttered that night. After all, what we ultimately share with others is shaped by and connected to the secrets we keep. In this way, I sense that Dad's unspoken recollections are still present in this document of scribbled notes, safely tucked away in the belly of words he spoke to me that evening. My father's muted memories are folded into his spoken memories, like delicate layers of tissue paper that stick to and bleed through one another.

················

In the immediate evenings following my father's death, I scoured the internet for evidential crumbs that could magically connect me to his family in North P'yŏng'an Province and P'yŏngyang. In hindsight, this reaction was a knee-jerk response driven by determination and desperation (a potent mixture) during a time of intense grief. Yet miracles can and do happen. Once, my dear friend Vinh visited an archive in California for his research on the life stories of Southeast Asian refugees. On his very first day in the archive, he found a photograph of his mother in a Thai refugee camp in a faded newspaper clipping from the 1980s. In that image, she stares directly at the camera and, by extension, at Vinh. In an interview, he recounts: "It was literally the second file that I opened, not even an hour into my first day in the archive.... It felt really surreal; just the shock of identifying yourself or your personal history in a larger history."[11] What Vinh experienced in that remarkable archival encounter is what I am hoping for as well: the utter shock of finding my family as part of a larger history. But even as I desire to see traces of my family within the annals of documented history, I know that official narratives enshrined within textbooks and public memorials are never neutral or objective. On the contrary, history is almost always crafted by victors and those who hold power. It is through the victor's framing that we learn, from an early age, whose lives matter, who is considered fully human, and which lives are grievable. Consequently, I've come to understand history as a genre of writing that troubles the boundary between fiction and nonfiction. History is an incomplete form of writing filled with strategic omissions.

During these nocturnal searches for my father's family, I come across websites that showcase prewar photographs of P'yŏngyang between the 1920s and 1940s. On one site, there are beautiful landscape portraits of serene lakes surrounded by mountain slopes and graceful Korean red pines, as well as aerial views of a city dotted with ancient Buddhist temples, railroad tracks, and a mix of Western-style architecture and traditional hanok-style buildings with their identifiable tiled roofs. These photographs portray an older version of P'yŏngyang that no longer exists. Between 1950 and 1952, my father's birthplace was leveled by American carpet bombing, with the most devastating raids in 1952 under a sustained attack that the US government refers to as Operation Pressure Pump. After 1953, with assistance from China and other socialist states, Koreans rebuilt the capital city with determination, even with the promise of future bombs from the United States.

Both of my sisters have been to P'yŏngyang at different moments: Cris in 2012 as part of Nodutdol's educational program, and Coleen in 2017 as a member of the global peace organization Women Cross DMZ. While US media often comment on P'yŏngyang's Soviet-style brutalist architecture with its massive concrete buildings unadorned by decoration, my sisters share with me softer sides of a city that I hope to visit someday.[12] In a poem Cris wrote for *Reencounters*, she remembers P'yŏngyang through snapshots that bring to life its leafy parks and the glimmering Taedong River during balmy summer nights. As I read the poem out loud, its words unspool like a hymn dedicated to my father's birthplace.

The Taedong River,
emerald and shadows.

Short-horned grasshoppers
wedding-air, distracting

couples who are stretching
their legs, lingering

near water—last days
of summer.[13]

Between looking at these photographs of P'yŏngyang and reading my sister's poem, I envision the circumstances of Dad's birth. By the mid-twentieth century, a convergence of influences ranging from Western missionaries and Japanese colonialism to socialist aid teams transformed the medical field in Korea through the construction of impressive hospitals and clinics.[14] Still, most women in the 1940s gave birth in their homes with support from 산파 (sanpa), or midwives, and elderly women referred to as 삼신 (samshin), named after the Korean goddess of childbirth and fate.[15] I can see my grandmother Jeongsuk as she navigates labor for hours and hours, drenched in perspiration as she curses from the unending pain. A choir of concerned grandmothers hovers over her, telling her to breathe and push; but she wants nothing more than to be left alone. Finally, there is a loud wail from both mother and baby as my father makes his way into the world. *He is finally here*, my grandmother sighs. As the midwife washes the baby and carefully wraps his fragile body in a large warm towel, Jeongsuk closes her eyes and drifts into deep slumber. All of a sudden, it is still and quiet, with only the lapping *plop* sounds from the Taedong audible from a distance.

The year of my father's birth, 1948, was a key moment in contemporary Korean history. Separate presidential and parliamentary elections were held in the southern and northern zones of the country, paving the way for two different governing systems—one capitalist (south), the other socialist (north). These elections were precipitated by earlier events in 1945, when World War II and Japan's four-decade colonial rule of Korea (1905–45) came to a dramatic close.[16] As it turns out, this ending segued with a different beginning: By September 1945, Soviet and US militaries swooped into the Korean Peninsula, the former occupying the north and the latter, the southern half. These mutual occupations portended Korea's positioning as a key battleground between two Cold War superpowers with competing visions for a new world order.

As early as 1947, skirmishes between local political factions, as well as civilian protests and massacres, spread throughout the Korean Peninsula and Jeju Island.[17] By June 1950, large-scale fighting erupted into what we now call the Korean War, engulfing soldiers and medical staff from more than twenty countries. Between 1950 and 1953, the US military dropped more bombs in northern Korea, 635,000 tons to be exact, than it did in the entire Pacific theater during World War II. Four million Koreans perished during this time, though civilian casualties are never mentioned in school curricula in the United States. On July 27, 1953, an armistice, rather than a permanent peace treaty, was signed by delegates representing the Korean People's Army (north Korea), the People's Volunteer Army of China, and the United Nations Command (UNC). This is significant because the armistice produced a pause to the armed fighting without ever ending the war. To this day, Korea remains frozen in suspended warfare, with two Korean states separated by a solidified border that severs the peninsula along the 38th parallel.

These historical details provide an anchoring point for me to sketch out the broad strokes of Dad's earliest years in Korea. It is these larger dynamics that ignited what would befall my parents' families and millions of other Koreans in the ensuing years. The 1948 solidification of a new international border in Korea created mass panic and paranoia as civilians migrated both north and south to avoid political persecution. Swollen numbers of Koreans recruited for colonial service and industrial and agricultural labor in Japan and Manchuria were still making their way home as well, which only added to the chaos. When mass-scale fighting erupted in 1950, additional waves of exodus followed as hundreds of thousands of civilians frantically escaped from artillery and aerial fire, fleeing across rivers, fields, mountainous passages, and seas. Escaping during the Korean winters was especially treacherous, as refugees trekked in subzero temperatures, often with little to eat and wearing thin layers of clothing made from materials like woven hemp.

While Dad never communicated any details regarding his family's migration to the south from P'yŏngyang, he mentioned to me during our conversation on his seventieth birthday that his family moved to Seoul in 1950. When I read about this early phase of the war in publications, I discover that the winter of 1950 was a particularly bruising period of fighting. By the autumn of that year, the Chinese and north Korean armed forces pushed the UNC and the Republic of Korea (ROK) military southward past the 38th parallel. This southward advance forced Korean refugees to flee active combat zones through coordinated evacuations from Hŭngnam's port in December 1950.[18] The bulk of those forced to leave never returned to their homes, and hundreds of thousands were separated from loved ones. This history touched my father's family as well. During their lifetimes, my dad and his family never returned to north Korea. They never saw the emerald glint of the Taedong River again or spoke with family and friends who chose to stay. When I consider this timeline, I realize that it is possible that my father and his family were a part of this stream of refugees who fled their homes via the Hŭngnam port in 1950. I envision my grandparents and their older children bundling what they could carry during the chaos of evacuation—perhaps a scattering of shirts and dresses, dried fish and fruit, and my grandmother's jewelry—in bogaji, or square cuts of hefty cloth used to wrap goods. My grandfather hugs and carries my two-year-old father, then his youngest child, on his back, tightly wrapping him with thick blankets to keep him warm in the unforgiving winter cold. *We're going on a long trip, Inki, so hold on tight*, my grandmother whispers to him. A lighthearted child who always believes what he is told, my father is excited about this unexpected adventure. He waves goodbye and blows kisses to his aunties, uncles, and cousins.

....

The Memory-Gift of the Taedong

As Jeongsuk stands on the cement edge of the Taedong River, a childhood memory resurfaces for her. She is six and sitting in a skiff with her father at dawn as he fishes for the flathead grey mullet in the river. At her parents' restaurant, the specialty is 숭어국, or sungeoguk, a steaming brothy soup made from the tender mullet along with a magical potion of black pepper, ginger, scallions, and garlic. Her father whistles a folk tune as he patiently waits for the tugging pull of the fishing line. Although it is chilly, Jeongsuk looks down and skims her fingers along the aqueous skin of the Taedong. It is finally April, and the river has recently thawed from a harsh winter. As she feels the slippery water on her fingertips, there is a tepid coolness that feels gentle rather than frigid. *The water feels like spring*, she says to herself.

What is beneath the river's shimmering surface? Once, Jeongsuk's mother told her about the mythology of Tan'gun, the revered founder of 고조선 (Kojosŏn), or Old Chosŏn, the first kingdom on the peninsula. As legend has it, Tan'gun was the son of the heavenly Hwanung and the bear-woman Ungnyŏ and established a walled city in the Taedong basin near the city of P'yŏngyang. The Taedong River, teeming with fish and kelp, became the source of life for this burgeoning community. But Jeongsuk's mother also cautions her with a concerned voice. *Be careful. There are monsters that make their home in the river.* When Jeongsuk catches mysterious creases in the river's surface, she wonders whether these creatures have emerged from the depths of the water to speak with her. *If they came to me, what would I say to them?* Even though her mother has repeatedly warned her about spending too much time by the water, Jeongsuk is not afraid. In fact, she is intrigued. She has so many questions! An only child with parents who worked all the time, she was always looking for new creatures to befriend.

Jeongsuk blinks and snaps back to the present. She is no longer a child but a young mother of four children. Even with her daughters, sons, and house helpers who stay with her while her husband is traveling for work (which is often), she feels alone. Once in a while, Jeongsuk returns to the river to shed secrets and to look for the hidden water creatures. She closes her eyes as she listens to the rhythmic ripples of the Taedong; it, too, longs to speak with her. *Where are you?* she inquires. Of all her children, it is her son, Inki, who resembles her the most. When she takes her children for walks along the river during the spring and summer, it is Inki who is the most enchanted by the water's mystery. While barely two years old, he intuitively gravitates toward the Taedong and is the only child who cries when they have to leave. She envisions his chubby face with its mischievous smile, and Inki's tendency to stealthily take things that don't belong to him, like the toys of his siblings. Though frustrating to encounter, his audacity makes her laugh out loud.

Instead of telling him stories about the river's monsters, Jeongsuk tenderly shares with Inki that the Taedong is full of possibility, even love. *It is here to protect us, son.* Inki's eyes widen as he giggles. After all, Tan'gun established life on the Korean Peninsula along the Taedong because he sensed that the basin was safe and could hold the abundance of life. This is the fairy tale she passes on to Inki, in the hopes that he, too, will one day share this version with others. Decades later on a different continent, it is Inki's youngest daughter, Mun-hye, who envisions her grandmother standing by a river that contains her guarded past. While Inki never shared this childhood story of the Taedong with her or her sisters, Mun-hye nevertheless receives it as a cherished memory-gift during sleep.

Jeongsuk sighs and clenches her fists. She is tired and doesn't want to leave. But she is late again, so she briskly walks home to prepare for her husband's return from a conference in Shanghai. Slowly turning her back to the river, Jeongsuk utters, *I will return soon.*

....

A year following my father's death, I received information that imploded the coherent narrative I had so proudly formulated about his family history. Through correspondence with academics and an intellectual biography written about my paternal grandfather by the Korean literary scholar Kim Yunsik, I discover that my grandfather Baik Cheol was an adamant supporter of the Japanese colonial administration after 1935.[19] This made his family a surveilled target of north Korea's anticolonial government and likely prompted a permanent move to the south before 1950. After I reviewed existing literature, this timeline makes sense given that my grandfather was already working in south Korea by 1948 as a full-time lecturer at Seoul National University and had established a family residence in the Seoul neighborhood of Anam-dong. Even after being celebrated for decades in south Korean literary circles, Baik Cheol's name is included in the notorious *Ch'in'il inmyŏng sajŏn (Encyclopedia of Pro-Japanese Figures)*, published in 2009. The dictionary includes the names of over 4,700 prominent writers, performers, public intellectuals, politicians, and entrepreneurs in south Korea accused of collaborating with the Japanese colonial regime between 1910 and 1945.[20] In a subsequent article published in the *Journal of Korean Language and Literature,* Baik Cheol is described by the author as an "opportunist" who "defected" to the south.[21] Again and again, I am confronted with this language of colonial collusion and complicity in the articles I read about my paternal grandfather.

As I digest this information, I am shaken. Years ago while I was still a graduate student, I had briefly corresponded with a professor who lauded my paternal grandfather's scholarship and described him as "one of the truly great literary critics of twentieth century Korea." Yet, at the conclusion of their message, this professor added, "It is true that some have accused him of 'pro-Japanese activities' in the late colonial period. I am not at all convinced that this is in any way a fair charge, but you should know that it does exist in some quarters."[22] While I was taken aback by this offhand comment, the celebratory tone of the email made it easier for me to shrug off this information as an embellished story. I convinced myself that this professor was offering a cautionary note so that I would not be hurt or offended if this rumor of colonial betrayal was ultimately communicated to me. For whatever reason, I never took the time to ask my father about this dark side of my grandfather's intellectual life, nor did I pursue this line of inquiry in my own research. Perhaps a part of me did not want to dig deeper because I feared what I might discover in the process.

But now that I am confronted with this well-documented history of undeniable collusion between my grandfather and the colonial regime, I have become uncertain about the reliability of Dad's memories. More specifically, the unearthing of this unsavory history makes me question the idealized recollections Dad shared about his father with my sisters and me. Throughout our childhood and into my graduate school days, my dad shared that as a young intellectual, Baik Cheol was fiercely *against* Japanese colonial rule. As I found out later in my research, my grandfather graduated from the Tokyo College of Education in 1927 and was imprisoned by the Japanese colonial government between 1933 and 1935 due to his participation in a Marxist literary organization, the Korean Artists Proletarian Federation (KAPF). He was, in fact, a core member of the KAPF.

Following his release, he publicly recanted his Marxist views, and his work pivoted toward a "humanist" bent. In an increasingly polemical world, he believed that literary critics needed to take a "neutral" stance in their scholarly writing. Beginning in 1939, he became a more vocal proponent of the Japanese Government-General of Korea, working as a reporter for its newspaper and promoting a literary association deferential to colonial rule. After the Korean armistice in 1953, Baik Cheol became a public intellectual in south Korea, becoming the first dean of the College of Liberal Arts at Chung-Ang University (1955–57) and retiring as the dean of the graduate school at the same institution (1972–73). He also held various teaching posts in the United States, including at Yale and Stanford. But to the best of my knowledge, this insinuation of colonial collusion trailed him for the rest of his life, creating resentment in some academic circles

Again, I return to my archived correspondence with the professor who first hinted at my grandfather's history of colonial involvement. When I reread their email, I appreciate how kind and careful they are with their words. I am curious, though, as to whether they were withholding biting critiques of Baik Cheol, like *Your grandfather betrayed his political commitments and people for the sake of writing again.* With the very little that I know about the personal stakes my grandfather juggled alongside his political activism, I attempt to take this news with a grain of salt. But, admittedly, I am gutted and wonder whether this turn of events shaped who my father would become. Did my grandfather's consequential choices compel my dad to choose an entirely different career outside of academia? Did Baik Cheol's desire for neutrality influence my father's political apathy? Did Dad grow up with any knowledge of his family in north Korea, or was he, too, raised in a house of forgetting?

The formality with which my dad spoke of his father—as an elder, an intellectual, and a professor—also gestures to an emotional distance that developed between parent and child. That is, while my dad spoke about his father with pride, his comments were limited to my grandfather's professional accomplishments. This sense of formality between my grandfather and father could have been a consequence of patriarchal norms that dictated that women raise their children while their husbands pursue public lives in order to support their families. But also: Given my grandfather's family in the north and his past association with Marxism, his absences from the home could have been an improvised form of protection that shielded his family from the threat of state surveillance. Or perhaps my grandfather's memories of colonial collaboration haunted him so much that he was unable to look into his children's eyes. As my father grew older, this emotional remoteness hardened into something else: disappointment, even a sense of resigned failure. A year after my father's death, my mother shared with me that he was considered the "black sheep" and the "disobedient one" in his family. *He was wild, he drank too much, and he refused to listen to his parents. Your grandfather felt heartache over this. Dad had a difficult relationship with Grandpa.*

....

If the tentative information I've gathered about my grandfather is patchy at best, I know even less about Dad's mother and his siblings. I have a single photograph of my grandmother's visit from Seoul when she stayed with us in Fountain Valley for several weeks when I was nine—the only time I remember meeting her. In that photograph, my mother is standing next to her, pale and thin, but smiling. In contrast, my grandmother, at least a head shorter than my mother, has a flat expression as she blankly stares at the camera. The only memory I have of this visit is my grand-

Despite these charges of collusion, I want to spend time with you, grandpa.

I want to ask you about your time in prison. I want to better understand the reasons for the seismic shifts in your thinking and writing. I want to know about the novels and poetry you read as a young person.

In my research on your life and work, I discover that you wrote several poems, including "Dongdoek!" in 1929, which reflected your original commitments to proletarian roots. The poem calls for the idyllic creation of a peaceful world through the collective labor of workers and farmers. I want to tell you that your granddaughters are writers — and that one of them is also a poet. As a young person, you dreamt about publishing a collection of poetry. I want to return with you to your humble birthplace, 의주 near the Chinese-Korean border, and walk across the land your family farmed. I want to ask you about your relationship with your eldest brother Se-myoung whom you were close to. I want to ask you about my father as well. What was he like as a child? I often think about his rebellious spirit and refusal to follow rules — I wonder whether this inspired or concerned you. I want to trace the lilting inflections and listen for the tonal similarities that suture your voice to that of your child's.

mother's uncanny resemblance to my father (her nose and stance, for example), alongside the bitter memories my mom shared before her visit.

While these stories belong to my mother and are hers alone to share, it is safe to say that the tensions between my mother and her mother-in-law were insurmountable. The sole biographical detail Mom ever disclosed to me about Dad's mother is that Choi Jeongsuk was the only child of merchants who managed a grocery store or small restaurant in Suwŏn before moving to P'yŏngyang.[23] Besides references in existing recollections to how beautiful she was and her vibrant youthfulness when she married my grandfather, I am still struggling to find other details about my paternal grandmother's life. Choi Jeongsuk's erasure from our family's memories is aided by my grandmother's working-class roots and gendered status as a woman, especially as the much younger, uneducated wife of a famous husband-scholar. Compounding this silence is the way in which mothers-in-law are often caricatured by Korean popular culture as petty figures who meddle in family affairs, with the daughter-in-law becoming the primary target of torment.[24] In addition to these larger dynamics that likely informed my mother's adamant refusal to speak about her mother-in-law, there are also unforgotten betrayals and acts of harm between my father's family and my mother that will never be disclosed to me.

But as much as I want to acknowledge and honor my mother's anger when she mentions my paternal grandmother, I also refuse to delimit Choi Jeongsuk's personhood to the constrained bounds of the terrible "monster-in-law." This descriptive flattening would only contribute to her status as evacuated from the family memory archive. Instead, during moments of solitude, I conjure her presence and the person she might have been before, during, and after her marriage to my grandfather. These moments of story emerge, not as part of a carefully crafted narrative, but as momentary visions that materialize, then fade, when I am close to bodies of water. During my long walks along an unpaved road that hugs a reservoir near my house, Jeongsuk suddenly appears before me. I can see her at a distance, standing along the muddy banks of the Taedong as she looks for pieces of sky reflected in the river's veneer. Her hair is neatly braided in one long strand down her back, while the slight breeze accentuates the crinkles in her stiff blue skirt, or chima. Our gazes never meet, but we can feel each other's presence.

When I observe the creases in her forehead, echoed by pursed lips that drop at the corners, I sense that my grandmother is longing to let go of secrets that only river monsters can hold. Or perhaps she is simply craving the smell and taste of sungeoguk. In these moments, time and space are invented: These beds of water in Southern California and Korea transform into portals where Jeongsuk and I coexist in the same realm. Walking past wild bushes of white sage and rust-colored buckwheat with the gravelly crunch of pebbles beneath my feet, I listen closely for the rough textures of my grandmother's voice and laughter. *Her voice is raspy and scratchy, and she laughs like my father.* In these brief encounters, I hesitate to ask Choi Jeongsuk how she felt about her grandchildren and whether she forgot about my sisters and me after she visited us in California for the first and last time.

The only truly verifiable pieces of information I have on my father's siblings are some of their names, which are cited in my grandfather's biography: Seunghye, Inae, Inkyeong, and Insu. Since my father never spoke about them to my sisters and me, I can only assume that they shared a volatile relationship with Dad. After my grandfather's death in Seoul in October 1985, sibling tensions exploded over inheritance decisions, or so my mother tells me. I am not privy to the fine print of this settlement, nor am I certain whether my mother's version of events is, in fact, what unfolded.

My mother tells me that due to confusion over visa restrictions, my dad did not return to Seoul following his father's passing. But at some point, Dad received a package in the mail with a VHS recording of the memorial service. Decades later, Coleen gifted Cris and me with digitized copies of this video. Though the sound in the recording is barely discernible and the images are fuzzy, I can make out dozens of people in their well-to-do suits, dresses, and hanbok, or traditional Korean attire. These steady streams of guests are seated behind a front row reserved for my grandmother, my father's siblings, and close family friends. Dad's sisters have donned funerary white hanboks, and his brothers are wearing the long yellow mourning hats worn by the sons of the deceased at Korean memorials. A circumference of trees encircles a building that guests enter before the outdoor ceremony, while the autumn sunlight intermittently hits the camera lens to induce faded scenes smudged by white heat.

While my first inclination is to dismiss my father's feud with his siblings as a petty squabble, I am reminded of what M, a friend, shared with me several years ago when we consoled each other over generations of conflict that have severed relationships in our families. The names of certain aunties, uncles, and cousins remain a mystery to us. Following

division, M's father and his family were forcibly removed from the farmland they collectively owned and worked for generations just west of P'yŏngyang. Facing extreme poverty, the family navigated their dispersal to the south by purchasing and reselling US military goods, such as canned goods and clothing, at inflated costs in the south Korean black market. The desperate desire for survival during a time of war and scarcity brewed conflict among these siblings. Decades after the fact, this strife spilled into the relationships of younger family members, forcing M to limit interactions with her cousins. Over the years, I have listened to different versions of the same story shared and reshared by friends and colleagues in the Korean diaspora.

M's sobering assessment reminds me of how the catastrophic losses of war beget more loss, mutating into a labyrinth of knotted intimacies we call family relationships.

....

아버지: THE FATHER-MAGICIAN WHOSE LAST ACT
WAS TO DISAPPEAR IN THE DUST OF SUNLIGHT

> I wonder if your adamant will to live, no matter the cost, was a resolute response to the circumstances of your birth.

I wonder if the lure of drinking came from a desire to access an un-
bridled freedom absent from your life.
I wonder if your decision to drive the Camry on that warm, bone-dry
Saturday
—wind kissing your hair as you closed your eyes and gripped
the steering wheel with determination—was a way for you
to touch this freedom.

....

In the days that followed my father's death, I received dozens of messages from friends and colleagues that conveyed their sincerest condolences for my family's loss. Several people shared with me that they hoped my memories of Dad would bring me joy, light, and laughter to mitigate the pain caused by his death. When I first read these comments, I didn't know how to respond. On the one hand, these messages buoyed me, and I appreciated the kindness afforded to my family and me. On the other hand, I felt alienated by the presumption that my relationship with my father would elicit a certain range of emotions. Many of my posthumous memories of Dad were not warm and fuzzy, nor did they evoke joy or light. Instead, they were immobilizing. The devastation I felt was not only because my father had passed away. I was also mourning for the life he didn't lead. In the following months, I continued to receive a stream of similar notes that were kind with good intentions. I began to wonder whether it was wrong for me to feel this way, and if there was space for me to share the contradictory feelings I had for my father, without diminishing the care and love I felt for him.

This unease was the initial impetus that compelled me to write about my father and his family history. I wanted to put into words, no matter how incoherent, a grief that felt ugly and convoluted. I wanted to create space for speculations that felt too uncomfortable to say out loud. Through writing, I've come to understand that my grief is not an emotional reaction to a single loss. Instead, it is a response to a longer history that stretches across the porous borders of time and space. This diasporic grief is in communion with the people of my everyday life, and with ancestors—relatives on both sides of my family, as well as rivers and land—I have never met. It precipitates from an arc of violence that molded who my parents and their parents became. The grief I harbor is also shaped by circumstances specific to my time and location. This distinction is important to make since my body is not an empty vessel through which silenced memories of my parents and grandparents are simply deposited. The grief I hold is my own, even though it is shared, relational, and contextual. In the most visceral sense, my diasporic grief emanates from the foreclosure of diasporic family relations in Korea and familial knowledges, as well as banishment and lost connections to land, language, and place. It is the heaviness I feel in the pit of my stomach when I know that the very best I can do is assume, conjecture, and imagine fragments that do not always fit.

But when I return to the wonderous optomap of my eye, I am reminded that grieving through writing has granted me entrance into another universe—an abundant cosmos full of contradictions and questions. Diasporic grief is capacious enough to hold divergent lines of family rumor, silence, and story. Though this meditative process has elicited more questions than answers, mourning through writing has permitted me to understand my father in ways that seemed impossible while he was alive. My writing is the improvised means through which I communicate with him. I tell him that I miss him and that I wish things could have been easier for him and for us.

whispers from a wind phone
                                      harnessed
                                by the pull of the moon

THE WIND PHONE

DEAR GRANDFATHER,

Several years ago, I learned of the wind phone, located near the coast of the Pacific Ocean in Iwate Prefecture. Sasaki Itaru installed a disconnected phone booth in his verdant garden, hoping that the wind would carry his bereaved voice to a beloved cousin he had lost to terminal cancer. Nestled along an edge between land and water, the wind phone is a zephyr bridge that connects the living to the dead.

In 2011, the Tōhoku earthquake and tsunami devastated Japan, sweeping twenty thousand lives into the aqueous folds of the Pacific. The ocean is a horizon that calms, as much as it engulfs and buries. That is the will of untamed water. Following the catastrophe, Sasaki offered the wind phone to survivors so they could hold communion with loved ones lost to this tragedy. To this day, survivors of the Great Earthquake continue to make pilgrimages to the wind phone. They dial the phone numbers of their parents, partners, siblings, children, friends, and lovers, mouthing their names before murmuring, *We miss you, we love you, we think about you every day.*

Sasaki shares, *The wind phone has become the grieving phone.*[1]

In my dreams, I visit the wind phone. It is the heart of winter. Snowflakes are falling onto my face, melting into porous skin that has been chapped by the unrelenting heat of Southern California. I have lived in the desert for too long. I enter the booth, breathing in and exhaling air that dissolves into evaporating clouds. Protected by thick walls of glass, I peer outside as mounds of white accumulate on the ground. From this place, I wonder if the wind would carry stories or silence to you.

Did I inherit my affinity for cold weather from you? My dad once told me that you relished bitingly chilly winters. In my few photographs of you, you are always dressed for the cold in your dashing jackets and scarves. In one image, you are wearing a wool cardigan with a cat sitting on your lap. I once read that you loved listening to the crunch of the snow beneath your boots as you made the solitary trek from Seoul to Sarang-ri, where your family lived during the war.

At this moment, these letters are a direct line to you, my wind phone. In bringing together shards of your life through writing, a hint of story emerges. Is this our diasporic family history? There are other things I would like to know. I want to know more about the consequential decisions you made. I want to know whether you loved your children. I want to know what became of your mother, your father, your brother. I want to read the utopic poetry you wrote as a young person. I want to know about the languages you spoke and forgot. I want to know what you hoped for and despised. I want to know whether you missed my father after he disappeared from your life. I want to know why my father lived and died the way he did.

But how, exactly, does one write to a ghost when there is no perceptible memory to call forth? Since these memories were never mine to begin with, I have no recollection of what I am searching for. They belong to you, and I have always only known you from a posthumous distance. You exist in parallel planes that have never touched and will never touch. You are real/a figment of my imagination. You loved my father/you held him at a distance. You are an ancestor/you are a stranger. What does remembering mean when the rehabilitation of memories is an impossible task? When I offer such questions, I am not seeking answers as much as I am acknowledging that these letters are addressed to you *and* to myself. Even if unanswerable, these queries provide a dwelling for names, bodies, and relations that have patiently waited to return to the living. "The realization of a life is often posthumous... waiting for its moment, and for us, in the future, which is so often a time and place that we... never reach."[2] Isn't this the heart of grieving—holding time and space for disappearances that will never be recovered?

Writing to you has been a disquieting process. I sense your unease with, even resentment about, stories I have shared on these pages. *There are things the living cannot talk about,* you tell me. On All Hallows' Eve, I am writing about your first son, whom you abandoned—I imagine a skinny teenager who searched for you up and down the peninsula as he escaped from terrifying air raids during the Korean War—and suddenly, the atmosphere surrounding my body shifts. A pressing heaviness settles onto my collarbones, tightening my shoulders and the eye of my throat; rustling sounds can be heard from the living room, even though I am alone in the house that I share with my husband, Dan, and our dogs. I hold my breath and turn my head away from the computer screen before asking, *Is someone here?* I am spooked. When I mention this to a friend the next day over lunch, they describe to me how Korean elders in their personal circle believe that on certain days, the barrier between the living and the dead dissipates into a permeable veil. *Ghosts walk among the living when they have unfinished matters they cannot let go of.* While chewing on my sandwich, I am struck by how familiar this story is to me; I have heard it before. When I was a child, my mother once told me that in Korean folklore, lamenting ghosts haunt family members, friends, and enemies when unresolved conflicts prohibit them from crossing the 황천길, the long bridge that stretches from the living realm to the underworld. This is most evident during special days like their death anniversaries and birthdays. *Remember to let go of anger, sadness, and all of your grudges before you fall asleep,* my mother cautions me.

That Halloween evening, while children in our neighborhood diligently roamed from house to house in their quest for candy, I lit incense and candles on my home altar. I asked for you to be at peace, and for my father to forgive me for how things ended. For several months, I stopped writing to you.

....

GRANDPA,

A year or so ago, I was gifted a copy of an intellectual biography about you, *A Study of Baik Cheol,* by Kim Yunsik. With help from a generous translator, I located two passages where your children are mentioned by name.[3] In the first passage, Kim writes that on December 16, 1950, you evacuated your home in Seoul with your family for Sarang-ri in Gyeonggi Province. "The family included daughters Seunghye and Inae, sons Inkyeong, Insu, and Inki."[4] By late fall 1950, stories circulated about the Chinese People's Volunteer Army's march south to recapture Seoul. A week before your departure from your home, your beloved brother Se-myeong unexpectedly appeared on your doorstep with his own son. They both looked exhausted, with smudges of caked dirt on their faces, and their lips were chapped from walking miles in the unrelenting snow. Se-myeong and your nephew intended to stay in P'yŏngyang, but ultimately, they retreated to Seoul and brought with them the news of the imminent arrival of Chinese forces.

From Elyse Semerdjian, a historian of the Armenian genocide I recently met, I learn of the word *telomere*. With roots in Greek, *telomere* is a composite between τέλος (telos), or "end," and μέρος (méros), or "part." An end-part. In the language of science, a telomere is the compound structure located at the tail end of a DNA chromosome. Scientists observe how chronic experiences of violence in one's lifetime shorten the length of the telomere, corresponding with a noticeable decrease in life span. *Violence is reflected by telomere time*, Elyse tells me. The etymological origins of scientific terms are so strange, and I find myself wondering how *telos* and *méros* coevolved to hold such consequential meanings of life and death.

The violence of telomere time. My father, your son, was not even three years old during your family's escape to Sarang-ri. I close my eyes to visualize how his tiny body absorbed the havoc as panicked neighbors fled their homes with only a few belongings in tow. How did his body respond when your family struggled to cross the Han River on a makeshift rubber boat during a snowstorm? How did his body respond to the percussive noise of denotating bombs that hit and incinerated entire villages? How did his body respond to the unease that followed for the next three years when your family did not know what the next day would bring? How did his nervous system process what was happening when he did not yet have the language to name the violence? This early time in my father's life was consequential. It stunted his ability to understand, react to, and accept things that harmed him and to acknowledge when he harmed others. When Dad's health started to deteriorate in his mid-fifties, his blood circulation weakened, his legs started to swell from water retention, and he was exhausted all the time. Yet he could not comprehend, or refused to comprehend, what was happening. For a long time, he could not confront the reality of his mortality and ignored the damaging effects that this denial had on his family. My mother took care of him in ways she shouldn't have had to.

Your children are mentioned a second time in *A Study of Baik Cheol* in your description of your commute back to Sarang-ri from Seoul:

> After passing through a small village called Omok-ri, climbing the long pathway in the valley known as Doduk-gol, walking over the ridge, traversing the extensive distance called Baran,

and navigating several more ridges again, then a small street called Choam appears. As mentioned earlier, you must follow the roads between rice paddies on the left side before reaching Choam-ri and cross over the hill to enter the village. This journey was a boring and challenging one, trudging along with a backpack for 60-ri.

Typically, as I ascended the final hill near Choam-ri, the sun had already set on those shorter days of fall, casting the mountain paths into darkness. However, I could picture my wife and little sons and daughters waiting for me—they would be sitting together, gathered under the warm glow of an oil lamp in Sarang-ri—like the warm light of the lamp to my eyes.

In this manner, I contemplated that my life may not be one that unfolds on a grand stage but rather follows a humble path of hope, akin to this narrow mountain road that I was walking by seeing the comforting glow of a lamp.[5]

My father isn't mentioned by his name in this passage, but your descriptive sketch provides a flickering image of him as a child. To this day, my sisters and I have yet to see a photograph of Dad at this tender age. Until I read this passage, I had never conceived of my father as a child, only as a fully formed adult. In the scene conjured by your words, my father is a four-year-old, pressing a rosy cheek against a frosted window. Anticipating your arrival with impatience, he drums his chubby fingers against the windowpane, making a *tap tap tap* sound that echoes, like drops of water, across the infinite expanse of winter.

....

While my father did not speak of you often when I was a child, his voice dropped an octave whenever he mentioned your name. His descriptions of you are respectful and polite, as if Dad was speaking about a revered elder rather than his own father. *Did you know that Grandfather was a famous scholar and writer? He was an important person in Korea and spent a lot of time in Europe and the United States.* There was a singularity to your name because you were the only person in his immediate family that my father spoke of. You were the lone survivor of banished memories that my sisters and I have never been able to access.

When I first read these excerpts from *A Study of Baik Cheol*, I was touched by the warmth of your words. "I could picture my wife and little sons and daughters waiting for me—they would be sitting together, gathered under the warm glow of an oil lamp in Sarang-ri—like the warm light of the lamp to my eyes." But as I revisited the passage a second and third time, a scratchy blockage emerged in my throat. Somehow, the descriptions do not align with Dad's descriptions of you, which were respectfully distant. In effect, my father's idealized descriptions of you repressed what he could not share about you with his daughters. This makes me curious about the parent you might or might not have been to your children. I wonder whether Dad confided in you or sought your guidance. Did you take your children on your trips abroad, which often lasted for months? Did Dad disappoint you or make you happy?

While my father loved us, he was never the parent my sisters and I longed for or needed. Since children learn and grasp through observation and experience, I've wondered whether you held and cared for Dad, or whether he was emulating what he observed and what was modeled for him. When I was in high school, my father shared something with me that I never disclosed to anyone except to Cristiana. It was late in the evening, and Cris and I had just returned home from dinner with friends. By then, Coleen was already at Wellesley College near Boston. As we entered the house, our parents were on the explosive heels of a heated argument and had just retreated to their respective corners. Our mother stormed into the bedroom while Dad briskly gathered his things to leave for the night. Partly hidden by the bathroom door, I peeked my head just beyond the door's edge to catch a glimpse of my father as he clenched his keys. Unexpectedly, we locked eyes as he gently said, *I'm sorry I don't know how to be a better father.*

....

For most of my life, my father was a living apparition. I began to mourn for my frayed relationship with him as a child. Even after we resumed communication following my return to Los Angeles in 2010, Dad and I exchanged niceties in Korean and English. Banal questions like "How are you?" and "How is the weather?" substituted for questions that were never asked. I am sharing this with you because you spent your entire life studying the volatile fault line that separates silence from language. What is birthed in this splintered space? What remains, what disintegrates?

Silence and language. Silence *as* language.

Korean was the first language I learned to speak, and the only language I spoke for the first five years of my life. This is where timelines of severance intersect: The deterioration of my relationship with my father is entwined with the deterioration of my Korean. Despite the loss of complete fluency, Korean has left a permanent mark and permeates cerebral crevices in ways that are mysterious. In Korean, surnames come before first names, verbs are inserted at the end of sentences, and gender pronouns are mostly absent. Korean is also a phonetic language, so words are enunciated the way they are spelled. These grammatical idiosyncrasies form a linguistic scaffolding through which I've come to learn and speak English *as my very own*. That is, my English is a vernacular language rather than a universal one. When I was younger, teachers assumed I did not have a firm grasp of English grammatical rules because I jumbled the order of adjectives, verbs, and nouns. During college, the supervisor of my work study job assumed I had dyslexia and recommended that I seek speech-language therapy. *You learned English as a second language, yes?*

Dad's presence-absence, too, makes itself known in quiet ways. He appears while I am washing dishes after dinner, during walks with our dogs on rainy days, and when I am driving home after a long day at work.

Silence and language. Silence *as* language.

....

GRANDFATHER,

When a friend emailed me a link to your profile on an academic website, I scanned the details that indicate when and where you were born, and when and where you passed away. My eyes fixate on the field where your name is provided. To my surprise, there are multiple names:

> Given name: 백세철 (白曘鐵) (Baek Se-cheol)
>
> Pen name: 백철 (鐵) (Baek Cheol)[6]
>
> Japanese name: 白矢鐵雄 (Shiraya Tetsuo)[7]

While Koreans were systemically forced to adopt Japanese names under the policy of sōshi-kaimei, I am uncertain when you took up Japanese as your own language. Your birth year of 1908 overlaps with the early years of Japan's gradual annexation of Korea. Soon after, Japanese became the lingua franca that Korean students were forced to think, converse, and write in during the colonial period. As was the case for Korean scholars, artists, and writers of your generation, I assume that Japanese was the primary language you spoke with your colleagues for several decades. During the arc of Japanese rule, what happened to Baek Se-cheol, and how did he become Shiraya Tetsuo?

In engaging snippets of your intellectual work and biography translated from Japanese and Korean into English, I learn of your political stance after 1935. The contradictions between your pre- and post-1935 political selves—from an active member of the Korean Artists Proletarian Federation (KAPF) to a colonial loyalist—are remarkable to me. A historian who contacted me a year ago through social media shared with me that in December 1938, you published a story of your political conversion in the *Dong-a Ilbo*. For the past nine months, I have searched digital collections and online archives, hoping to find a copy of this publication, without success.

When I first learned of your past, I was stunned, then angry at and ashamed of this family history. Previously, I had spoken of you with pride, describing you to friends as someone I felt close to because of our shared anticolonial commitments. I resented my father for never revealing your past to me. But at times, I have doubts about whether your son, or any of your children, knew about this history. Other times, I can imagine why our father kept your story from us. He was skilled when it came to holding secrets; he knew what to disclose and what to keep to himself. He wanted, I think, to protect your identity as a prominent scholar and to pass on to his daughters this pristine memory as an untainted heirloom—one of the few things he could provide us with. Your mythic stature is a tall tale we grew up with in our household. My sisters and I adored you.

As disheartening as your story is to me, there is so much I don't know and am still learning. It would be so easy to disavow you and write about your life and work with dejection. But I cannot relegate your experiences to stagnant binaries, such as good/bad, because they fail to hold the contradictions of who we are. In my research, I have read about bilingual Korean scholars and writers during the Japanese colonial period, and the schizophrenic self-divisions they internalized as they confronted their "Korean-ness" through policies enforced by the Japanese government. In a solemn letter addressed to his mother, the writer Kim Saryang, your younger compatriot from P'yŏngyang, requests that his sister translate his letter from Japanese into Korean so that their mother could read the letter. Throughout his short life, Kim wrote of his intense alienation from Korean *and* Japanese as he struggled to know and express himself through these tongues. In contemplating this agonizing impasse, Nayoung Aimee Kwon writes in *Intimate Empire: Collaboration and Colonial Modernity in Korea and Japan*, "The chasm between mother and son is unbridgeable. The opportunities promised Kim (and other Korean male intellectuals in this new colonial world) distance him further from his own mother and from his mother tongue."[8] After Japanese colonial rule abruptly ended in 1945, Koreans were directed to suppress, even forget, the Japanese language, as if the annihilating violence of colonial indoctrination never occurred.

In my attempt to make sense of your political conversion in 1935, I take this context into account. I don't forgive or absolve you for what happened and the chain of decisions you made. Instead, I want to better understand the relations of power that determined the options available to you. In prisoners' firsthand accounts reprinted in scholarly texts, I have learned how "disloyal" colonial subjects incarcerated at colonial prisons, like the one in Jeonju where you spent a year and a half, were starved, tortured, sexually assaulted, and disappeared. While I have yet to read about your arrest and imprisonment, it is not difficult to imagine how this damaging experience persuaded you to recant what you had worked so hard to seed and grow during your earlier life. To survive the totalizing violence of colonial brutality, you renounced your political and intellectual commitments, as well as your comrades. Out of intense fear, cowardice, or a desperation to write again, you chose to live another day with the unforgiving burden of betrayal, rather than die with a clear conscience. Did you feel guilty about this decision? What did it mean to be Korean at this time, and what did writing mean to you? My father spoke about your scholarship in broad strokes. In fact, he mostly celebrated your status as a prominent literary critic and published author in south Korea. At the end, I suspect that Dad knew very little about your field of study and the changing political orientations of your work. Perhaps you made the intentional decision to never disclose this part of your life to your children as a protective gesture.

Somewhere in the virtual realm of online forums, social media outlets, and Korean scholarly publications, I am certain there are contradictory responses to these questions. But I take my time in searching for you, titrating this process of information retrieval so I am prepared for what I may ultimately find.

....

Word: 친일 (ch'inil)

Meaning: Intimacy with Japan, colonial traitor, collaborator

Ch'inil, or intimacy with Japan, encompasses the ways that Koreans internalized feelings of resentment, fear, and social inferiority during Japan's four-decade rule. For colonial subjects caught within the labyrinth of imperial violence, *ch'inil* describes the affective geography of self-loathing and desire affixed to the fight for a place at the colonial table, no matter how peripheral or minor. This was especially true for Korean scholars, teachers, and writers, like you, who daily interacted with Japanese intellectuals at work, in schools, at restaurants, and in neighborhoods. You yearned to freely study, write, travel, and engage in intellectual dialogue as they were able to. Ch'inil is the zone of suffocating encounters, where the boundary between survival and complicity, and repulsion and yearning for the colonized and colonizer, becomes muddled.

I wonder what you gave up for these privileges.

....

GRANDPA,

The other day, my mother reminded me that you were the one who named me following my birth in Seoul. You named all your grandchildren. According to my parents, my first name, 문혜, is a derivative of the Korean word for the humanities, or 인문학. In 1984, my parents voluntarily relinquished 문혜 on my behalf when I arrived in the United States as a four-year-old. Uncertain what my name in the United States should be, my mother turned to her sister Kyung for guidance. In the possession of a book of English names, Auntie Kyung efficiently plucked three names from a single page: *Coleen, Cristiana, Crystal*. Suddenly, I became Crystal.

I am embittered by this name. Even after forty years of being called Crystal, this name has never belonged to me. It is an awkward fit, a second skin I never asked for nor wanted. When my first-grade elementary school teacher called Crystal during the daily roll call, there were times when the name did not register, and I would fail to respond. She would patiently pronounce this name, syllable by syllable, as if I could not hear or understand English.

C-R-Y-S / T-A-L, I see you in the front row. Please raise your hand.

To put it simply, I didn't recognize this name. During these moments, I desperately wanted to crawl beneath my desk and disappear. The other children would stare at me and snicker. *That dumb Chinese girl doesn't even know her own name.*

....

When I began to search for you, I learned that my grandmother, Choi Jeongsuk, was your fourth and last wife. When you married her in 1943, she was nineteen, and you were thirty-six. In biographical accounts, my grandmother is described as vibrant and youthful, and your wedding day as hot and sunny. The ceremony lasted just over an hour. When and where did you first meet Grandmother? Did my father resemble her?

As newlyweds, Grandmother and you departed for Beijing, where you lived, off and on, from 1943 until 1947. I'm hesitant about the timeline, but for now, it is the one I've managed to pull together from your biography, translated articles, and a colleague's speech given during your memorial service. I imagine that your stay in Beijing was a tumultuous yet buoyant one. Decades later, your memories of Beijing are bittersweet. Even during a time of war and rapid industrial change, you felt rejuvenated by the city's vastness and the vibrancy of its creative life (so many writers, painters, and an extraordinary theater life!). There was a small but established circle of Korean intellectual comrades you had known during your P'yŏngyang and Tokyo days; they welcomed you into their discussions and debates at local teahouses and restaurants. While you never shared this with your wife, you were resolute in your desire to stay. I close my eyes and imagine the noisy neighborhood you lived in, the winding streets you traversed, and the people, sounds, and scents you encountered.

Recently, I discovered that you were initially transferred to Beijing in 1943 by the *Maeil Shinbo*, a media organ of the Japanese colonial government, to oversee their local branch and staff. During these long years, you pursued part-time teaching work at the Women's Normal University and maintained a disciplined work schedule, committing at least three hours of your early morning to reading and writing. Two years following the end of the Asia-Pacific War, you acquiesced to your colleagues' adamant requests and returned to the peninsula with my grandmother, uncertain what and who you would find in Seoul. Eventually, you became a full-time lecturer at Seoul National University, transitioning into a rigorous work schedule while leaving your wife to care for your sons and daughters. And in December 1950: War refused to disappear from your life, as bombs forced your family to hastily evacuate your home in Seoul. Somewhere in your biography, I remember reading that your close friends from Beijing, the Zhangs, were visiting you in Seoul and that they, too, barely escaped from the punishing bombing raids that almost killed your entire family.

Certain decisions, no matter how arbitrary, will radically alter the course of our lives. With that said, I often wonder what would have happened if you had chosen to remain in Beijing with my grandmother. Would my father have been conceived in Beijing? If so, I wonder if his life would have fared better than what awaited him in Seoul and Los Angeles. Or maybe he would never have met my mother, placing my own fate, along with the fate of my sisters, in jeopardy.

After my father's death, I have dreamed about these divergent pathways that could have been. I know that my sisters, too, have envisioned my father's other lives. In a social media post, Cristiana shared a touching message about Dad after he disappeared, conjuring the life he led in a parallel universe. In this other reality, Inki Baik never married Young Ok Kim or had any children. He lived in harmonious solitude, happily surrounded by a forest of majestic oak and pine trees. He cared for injured animals, tending to them until they were healthy. He sipped whiskey in the evening with the windows cracked open, listening to Franz Schubert's "Du bist die Ruh" ("You Are Rest and Peace") on the record player with the pianissimo music slipping into the coolness of the nighttime air. In *this* life, my father, Inki Baik, was content and lived the way he wanted.

"THE WAY OF WRITING (PILBEOB)," FROM 동경대전 (*THE GREAT SCRIPTURE OF EASTERN LEARNING*)

The way of writing is attained by spiritual training. The reason for it is in one mind. The tree is a symbol of our country. Three times our nation almost reached the end of its destiny, but all was not totally lost. Since I was born in the East and realized the Way of the East, I will work for the East first. People have different minds, but I shall love all of them and make transparent and fair rules of life. With a peaceful mind and right energy one can draw a line, and all the Truths may be found in that one point. First, one must make one's writing brush soft and grind the black ink tablet many times, and then one can write. One must select thick paper to write on. There is a difference between great and small Truths. One should begin to write first with a solemn attitude and correctly, and then make the shapes like great mountains and lofty rocks.⁹

....

GRANDFATHER,

The day of your passing in October 1985, my parents lit incense by the foot of our front door and opened all the doors and windows to the house. My father stood by the doorway with a hunched back, a hand pressed against a wall to support the entirety of his weight. I was only five years old then and had never witnessed my father crying until that moment. He had always seemed invincible to me, but at that moment, he looked small and fragile. My mother knelt by me and whispered in my ear, *Grandfather's spirit departed, and he needs safe passage from this place.* I nodded as if I understood what was happening.

After my own father passed away, I searched for Korean funerary rituals to facilitate a safe passage for him. In the process, I discovered your family's formidable ties to Ch'ŏndogyo, a Korean indigenous religion that originated in the Tonghak or Eastern Learning peasant rebellion of the nineteenth century.¹⁰ Drawing from Confucianism, Buddhism, Taoism, and shamanism, Ch'ŏndogyo is rooted in the belief that the divine is inseparable from the human and our surrounding nature.

What I find the most alluring about Ch'ŏndogyo is not the religious tenets themselves but its history of anticolonial refusal. Ch'ŏndogyo first emerged in Korea in adamant resistance to Western religions brought to Korea by white Christian missionaries and Anglo and French colonial influences in Northeast Asia. It played a key role in the March 1st Korean Independence Movement of 1919, with key members fervidly organizing underground activist cells. In present-day north Korea, Ch'ŏndogyo is considered a radical revolutionary religion and is an existing component of national politics. Your biographical writing foregrounds how Ch'ŏndogyo remained a potent influence in your daily life. It provided an ethical compass to comprehend the world, as well as a supportive community that extended beyond your home. It was a Ch'ŏndogyo congregation that provided a scholarship for you to study abroad in Japan, and you attended Jongriwon, a Ch'ŏndogyo church, while residing in Tokyo as a student. Ch'ŏndogyo was also your mother's faith, and you were devoted to her. When she passed away in P'yŏngyang on September 14, 1949, you were devastated and mourned for her for over a year. I long to learn more about your relationship with your mother, and your reasons for leaving your home in Korea in the first place. I'm uncertain whether you ever had plans to return.

When I learn of your adherence to Ch'ŏndogyo, more questions about your political conversion surface. In your early twenties, you were a passionate member of the Ch'ŏndogyo Youth Party, writing idyllic poetry about Korean workers and farmers toiling for a socially just and equitable world. During this early period, you believed that socialism and Ch'ŏndogyo, or politics and religion, were inseparable. In a translated article, I learn that several scholars have addressed these contradictions by considering how core principles of Ch'ŏndogyo impacted your writing throughout the arc of your academic career.[11] Even before your political conversion, your literary criticism advocated for a serene balance, or neutrality, between what you perceived as earthly polemics.

Several months ago, I purchased a copy of the Ch'ŏndogyo Scripture (the *Donggyeong Daejon*), translated into English as the *Great Scripture of Eastern Learning*. A slim and elegant collection, the book is divided into the briefest of chapters. When one thumbs through its pages, the whimsical section titles read more like mythical poetry than religious principles. I am surprised by how moved I am by the lyrical text. In one of the earliest segments, titled "Poems, Incantations, and Other Writings," my eyes land on the chapter "The Way of Writing": "People have different minds, but I shall love all of them and make transparent and fair rules of life. With a peaceful mind and right energy one can draw a line, and all the Truths may be found in that one point."[12] Maybe this means that multiple, even contradictory, realities can coexist at a single point if we open ourselves to this possibility.

Reading these lines a century after you first engaged them, I imagine you were drawn to these pages precisely because they approach writing as a reverent act. This is a commonality that connects you to me, me to you. I, too, am drawn to writing as a corporeal act and sacred practice. "First, one must make one's writing brush soft and grind the black ink tablet many times, and then one can write. One must select thick paper to write on." This passage is about the purpose of writing in relation to spiritual training and the fate of Koreans as a people; writing is a spiritual practice with consequences and stakes beyond individual yearnings. During the last years of your life, you returned, again and again, to these lines. They comforted you as you sought refuge in a world that refused to provide you with the quiet and peace you longed for.

Although Ch'ŏndogyo was an integral part of your life, my father never mentioned this to me once. Did you share this part of your life with your children? In the last decade of his life, Dad remained steadfast in his own rituals. While he never attended church during this time or spoke about Christianity, his first act in the morning and his last act in the evening was prayer. Without fail, he would sit alone at the dining room table with his clasped hands folded over a Bible, mouthing whispered words that no one could make out. At times, I have wondered what he hoped and prayed for, and whether these daily invocations were something he observed and learned as a child from your devotional practices as a Ch'ŏndogyo follower.

....

DEAR GRANDFATHER,

Last week, the earth experienced a total solar eclipse where the entirety of the sun is momentarily blocked by the moon's spherical body. Los Angeles does not lie in the eclipse's path of totality, or the 115-mile narrow arc through which a total eclipse can be viewed, so the eclipse here was only partial. In the evening, I glanced at online photographs as boisterous crowds in Burlington, Buffalo, and Austin viewed the darkened sky in awe from parks, stadiums, backyards, and abandoned cornfields.

While the eclipse lasted for two and a half hours, the moon completely covered the sun for a mere four minutes. In this brief window of time, magical things happened. The day transformed into night, dropping the temperature by ten degrees. The gravitational pull of the moon shifted the rhythmic pattern of ocean tides. Fireflies became visible with their flickering bellies. In newspapers like the *Los Angeles Times* I read about the startling responses elicited by the eclipse. Some observers shared how they abruptly wept, while others laughed.

Others watched in silence as they attuned to the subtlest of movements and sounds. When I asked Coleen over the phone about her experience of the eclipse in New York, she responded in a whisper, "All I could feel and hear was the wind brushing against my arms."

During this celestial event, I wonder what else was released. In Korean mythology, an eclipse symbolizes the unlocking of the shadow world accompanied by an intensification of spiritual energies. The kingdom of darkness sends its ferocious bulgae, or fire dogs, to retrieve the sun and the moon. The eclipse is an indication of the dogs' bite marks. On their Instagram account, a Korean shaman, or mudang, shares how the eclipse provides a way to encounter, even to speak with, ancestor spirits. But they are also careful and cautious with their words; the mudang recommends that those who are sensitive to their surroundings carry protection with them.

The solar eclipse evokes other shadow myths from my childhood. When I was in second grade, an awful teacher once told me that monsters camouflaged themselves in dark shadows to hide among the living. When children failed to obey their teachers, these monsters would make their presence known, eating children with their viciously gnarled teeth. For a long while, this story petrified me and fueled nightmares that didn't subside until years later.

During the early morning of the eclipse, I sit alone in my living room, mesmerized by the kaleidoscope of light and shadows cast across the floor. This time, I don't look for the buried shapes of vengeful monsters. I instead search for silhouettes of ghosts I never said goodbye to. I look for you and your son, meditating on what I will say to you before the fire dogs steal the sun.

어머니 ‖ MOTHER

A COOKING LESSON.

YOUNG OK BAIK'S RECIPE FOR 미역국
(MIYEOK-GUK, OR SEAWEED SOUP)

INGREDIENTS

1 ounce miyeok (dried brown seaweed)

1–2 teaspoons salt

6 cups water

1 pound sliced beef, preferably beef brisket

Toasted sesame oil (preferably Kadoya or Ottogi)

Thinly sliced garlic (3 cloves)

DIRECTIONS

Wash and drain the seaweed, then soak in cold water for 10 minutes. Cut seaweed into 1-inch pieces.

Briefly sauté beef in a skillet with 1–2 teaspoons of toasted sesame oil and sliced garlic for 6–7 minutes. Add a tablespoon of water if beef starts to burn. This step of searing is important because it will enrich the savory flavor of the soup.

Place softened miyeok into a large pot with 6 cups of water and the salt and turn the heat to high. Let the water boil for 5 minutes, pot covered.

Add sautéed beef and garlic to the boiling water and after a minute, bring the heat down to simmer and cook for 40–50 minutes (covered). At the 40-minute mark, check to see if the beef is thoroughly cooked and tender.

Ladle soup into warm bowls. If necessary, add a touch of sesame oil for additional flavor (but don't add too much because it will make the soup unnecessarily oily).

Uhm-ma is in her kitchen, her tiny figure buzzing around as fragrant sesame oil snaps and sizzles in the frying pan. Her voice is bubbly bordering on boisterous—the usual animated tone it takes when she is cooking. Donning her flower-patterned apron as she deftly moves from the stove to the sink, Uhm-ma uses my Korean name when she speaks to me. *Mun-hye-ya, this is really good. You only use baby seaweed, this Korean brand, for miyeok-guk, okay? White brands are no good. Put this in cold water for 10, maybe 15 minutes. You listen, right?* As the nutty aroma of the sesame oil fills the air, Uhm-ma's voice overlaps with the *whoosh* of water as it spills into the pot and a *rip* as she tears open a bag of seaweed. Shelly, my parents' elderly dog, is excited by the commotion and peeks her fluffy head into the kitchen. I rub her chin before she grumpily circles back into her bed, irritated that we interrupted her beauty sleep. Uhm-ma and I giggle together.

....

When my mother began to show signs of depression in August 2022, my sisters and I weren't entirely alarmed. We had grown up with intermittent periods of Mom's sadness throughout our lives. These episodes were uneven, varying in time and severity. Many times, when we were in elementary school, before she started work with my father at a gas station, Mom would sleep for hours on a yo, or a thin floor mattress, in the living room with a cotton blanket pulled over her shoulders. She slept so soundly that I would often place my small, round face next to hers to ensure she was still breathing. During these stretches of comatose rest, my sisters and I would gather around her like a concerned flock of chicks surrounding a sick hen. We'd bring her hot yujacha, or honey citron tea, to soothe her nerves and would take turns rubbing her feet. On her request, we'd weed out strands of white hair from her head with tweezers, forming a pile of snow-colored filaments. Eventually, without fail, Mom would move out of these hazy moments and resume her daily schedule as if nothing had happened. Even during her most difficult spells, she made sure we ate, attended our school award ceremonies, and helped us with our algebra homework. She relished math because no matter how tricky the problem sets were, there were always clear-cut solutions. Mom, I think, longed for the same crystalline elegance in her own life, which was filled with uncertainty.

But during this most recent bout of depression, things were different. Days of feeling low turned into weeks, and weeks of drowsy napping turned into months. By late November 2022, her depression evolved into something I did not recognize. It became difficult for Mom to hold a coherent conversation for more than a few minutes. She couldn't maintain steady eye contact, and she started using body gestures—slapping her hands hard against her thighs or butting her head hard against my own—to communicate. I took her to see her doctor, who couldn't find anything physically wrong though he recommended therapeutic intervention and medication, which she adamantly refused. Naively, I relied on tricks that in the past had coaxed Mom back from a depressive cliff. I brought over homemade ddak juk, or chicken porridge; picked up her favorite groceries from H-Mart; slept over to keep her company; and took Mom to local parks and bakeries to lift her mood. My sisters Coleen and Cris took turns ordering favorite meals for my parents and coordinated rides for my father's dialysis appointments to lessen my caregiving load. As things worsened, my sisters and I held increasingly panicked discussions on Facetime to hammer out emergency and long-term plans. We navigated the byzantine maze of Medicaid and Medicare, attempting to find therapeutic support for our mother and assisted living facilities for our father. Finally, a Korean therapist my mother briefly spoke with over the phone urged me to seek professional intervention as soon as possible. *Your mom isn't getting better. She needs help.*

In the early morning of December 2, 2022, my father called to tell me that my mother was vacillating between moments of lucidity and complete incoherence. *Ah-ba, put Uhm-ma on the phone*, I directed Dad as calmly as I could. When I spoke with Mom, she was using a high-pitched voice, as if she was ventriloquizing a child's voice. *Crystal, my good girl. You won't put Mom away, will you?* Her voice then deepened. *Don't you come here, or Mom will disappear.* While I was making my way to my parents' home on the 10 East freeway, Coleen had already called the San Bernardino County crisis line for emergency intervention. At 10:47 a.m., my mother was accompanied by a police officer and social worker to a psychiatric facility on an involuntary hold. Holding my clammy hand and attempting to soothe me, the social worker shared that there was a credible fear that my mother would hurt herself, my father, or me without intending to. Standing on the sidewalk, I watched as my mother hit the passenger window of a white county van with clenched fists. She was desperate for an escape. The force of her rhythmic blows made me fearful that she would shatter the glass and cut herself. *Uhm-ma, I'm going to come get you as soon as I can, I promise.* As if viewing a surrealist film from a distance, I suddenly saw my father magically appear on the front porch. His mouth opened and shut, but no words could be heard. His wispy figure, almost like a ghostly shadow, melded with the wooden flesh of the door.

This was the last time my parents saw each other.

....

When asked in an interview about whether writers have the right to tell the stories of their family, Viet Thanh Nguyen responds, "We have no right. Anyone who tells these kinds of stories has to grapple with the ethics, the aesthetics, and the politics of what it means to tell this story."[1] But in *A Man of Two Faces: A Memoir, a History, a Memorial*, Nguyen *does* share the stories of his parents, including his mother's hospitalization on a psychiatric ward three times during her life. He recognizes the dilemmas associated with such sharing, and the consequences that each writer must bear as they discern what to disclose and what to keep off the page. *I have no right. I have to live with that.*

The subtitle of Nguyen's book, *A Memoir, a History, a Memorial*, gestures to why he chose, after all, to write about his parents' lives. His book does not focus solely on his parents but rather on the historical conditions that led to his family's resettlement—alongside hundreds of thousands of other Vietnamese refugees displaced by war, militarized raids, and bombs—in the United States. For me, the uncomfortable sense that Nguyen is transgressing a line he shouldn't be crossing eases when he matter-of-factly states that his family's story is knitted within the abhorrent history of American nation building, one enabled by settler warfare, genocide, and exploitation. Nguyen observes that no matter how seemingly personal, our diasporic family stories are *always* historical narrations that detail, on an intimate scale, how everyday life coheres, and in some cases falls apart, in the United States.

Nguyen's commentary has remained with me as I have written about my family. While I am more hesitant than Nguyen as to whether I should share my family's stories, I, too, consider my parents' lives as lines within a historical tapestry that bears the patterned marks of colonialism, war, and state violence. Admittedly, the stakes of sharing these stories vary for me, depending on who I am writing about. In the case of my father's estranged family, there is a totalizing absence that cuts two ways: On the one hand, piecing together his story has felt akin to making my way out of a canopied forest with little guidance. At the same time, this absence has allotted a degree of freedom where I do not have to negotiate family pressures when writing about subjects considered unsavory or taboo. But with my mother's family, the task of writing is a matter not of estrangement but entanglement: It is delicately nestled within a mesh of relationships with aunties, uncles, and cousins. Several cousins, my mother, and at least one of her sisters and brothers are aware I am writing this book. They have answered questions in person, as well as over the phone and email. While my mother's siblings have done their best to share what they can, pauses in their speech hint that they are considering what is safe to communicate. One of them requested that I omit from public writing specific memories they shared about their childhood in Korea, which I have respected to the best of my ability. Although these memories are missing as text, they are crucial to my mother's becoming in the world and have contoured the stories I share in these pages. As an undercurrent, these memories are *here* in their absence.

These conversations with family have made me cautious not to overstep with too many questions. But they have also made me determined to better understand the social worlds my mother and her family were a part of following the end of Japanese colonial rule and the beginning of US occupation. This tension between the desire to suppress and the longing to tell forms the backbone of my writing, from the selective memories I share, to the ways I write about my mother's earlier days in Korea—before she met my father, before she became a parent, before she migrated to the United States. Most important, it gestures to a question that exists at the heart of diasporic grief: How might we draw on language and silence to reckon with the dead, while also grieving for the living who remain tethered to pasts that refuse to let them go?

This fusing between the past and present has produced a sense of ambiguity around my mother's depressive ideation, a condition she has navigated ever since I could remember. Following her psychiatric hold in 2022, my sisters and I tried our best to grasp the depth of our mother's sadness. A flurry of doctors and psychiatrists offered contradictory diagnoses about her cognitive break, ranging from clinical depression with psychosis to clinical depression without psychosis to delirium to early-onset dementia and Alzheimer's disease. After speaking with six psychiatrists and physicians within a span of two months, I assumed that my mother's progression into madness was a consequence of taking care of my father for so many years, alongside the unresolved bitterness she held toward him during their marriage. Just as a tree branch snaps when it can no longer hold a burgeoning weight, my mother could no longer care for my father. She needed to disentangle her life from his presence, no matter the cost. Disassociation, it seems, was the easiest way to do this. After his death, I became furious with my father for the cumulative toll his actions had taken on my mother's life and personhood.

To accept what had befallen my mother, this is the explanation I provided myself with. I needed closure to quell my anxiety. But I later realized that this pathologizing diagnosis identifies my parents as the *sole* sources of the problem. It places onus on my mother to overcome an illness with gnarled roots in damaging social and familial systems. As I have learned from disability justice activists and scholars like Mia Mingus, Leah Lakshmi Piepzna-Samarasinha, and Mimi Khúc, struggles with chronic illnesses like post-traumatic stress disorder (PTSD) and depression are never about individual bodies per se.[2] Rather, they are intimately tied to asymmetrical conditions of violence that produce disproportionate levels of vulnerability for some, including working-class and poor women of color. These conditions range from overexposure to toxins, and limited access to health care and networks of support, to the ways that certain bodies are *always* perceived as dangerous, improper, and debilitated.

Seven months following my mother's hospitalization, I rediscovered a nearly forgotten audio recording that provided more family context for Mom's cognitive break. The file is fairly short, spanning just over twenty-four minutes, and was made on October 3, 2021, on my iPhone. In the recording, my mother is sharing her recipe for miyeok-guk with me, a savory seaweed soup usually made from beef broth. Traditionally, Koreans make miyeok-guk for a loved one's birthday, as well as for those who have recently given birth, to replenish them with nutrients lost during the birthing process. Legend has it that Koreans first began to make miyeok-guk when divers observed how whales fed on lush oceanic forests of seaweed after giving birth to their calves. This cooking lesson is motivated by a specific occasion: In a few weeks, Cris will give birth to her first child, Iseul. Since Mom is taking care of Dad, she is unable to travel to Oakland to support Cris during the postpartum period. Therefore, I am sent in my mother's place as a substitute caregiver, the one who must cook miyeok-guk for my twin sister. I am aware of the significance of this task and diligently record my mother's recipe because I don't want to forget what she shares.

When I listened to the recording for the first time, I was surprised by how little I remembered from our conversation. *How could I have forgotten about this recording?* In our talk, Mom provides directives on how much water, meat, and seaweed to use in the miyeok-guk. *Be sure to stir those pieces of beef well into the pot of seaweed and water.* But my mother and I are also conversing about her relationships with her parents and siblings when they lived in Korea, topics I've gingerly taken up with her over the years. I write "gingerly" because most of the time, I've sensed that Mom felt uncomfortable sharing details from her childhood. During previous occasions when I peppered her with questions— *Where were your parents from? Why did they come to Seoul? Why did you migrate to the United States?*—Mom skillfully changed the subject or simply said, *I don't remember, that was too long ago.* Other times, her response hinted at things she didn't want to say out loud. *Why do you want to know about a past that's no good?*[3]

In part, my mother willingly shares these memories because they are mediated through a family recipe, a sensual form of memory keeping bursting with tastes, textures, and smells. These memories can be excruciating, but they can also be full of vibrancy and nostalgic pleasure. Recipes remind us of our loved ones' creativity and resourcefulness amid their survival. As Grace Cho beautifully shares in *Tastes Like War*, cooking and eating always take center stage when she remembers her mother because food was a source of comfort *and* tenacity: "By returning to the scene of eating, I discovered not only things that broke her but also things that kept her alive."[4] For my own mother, cooking was not only a way of providing for her children when she couldn't afford to buy us fashionable clothes and shoes; it was also one of the few times she felt comfortable enough in her own skin to speak with us in Korean. When I would cook dinner with my mother during my visits, she would share colorful stories of how she bonded with her mother through the embodied pleasure of cooking and eating. *Your grandma was the best cook. She always chose the freshest vegetables and created her own recipes. Her jap-chae and galbi were chego (the best).*

Every now and then, my mouth waters when I remember the simple yet delicious dishes my mother made for her daughters, waking up at three o'clock every morning before she left for work. In the solitude of the kitchen, Mom cooked fragrant panch'an like gamja bokkeum (shoestring cuts of sautéed potato), spicy pickled cucumbers, various kinds of chigae depending on the season (meat and vegetable stews), and p'ajŏn (battered and fried vegetable and/or meat pancake). When I remember these dishes, I realize how much I miss my mother and her cooking.

TRANSCRIBED EXCERPT FROM COOKING LESSON WITH MOM | OCTOBER 3, 2021

(*Sounds of metal pots clanging*)

CRYSTAL: Uhm-ma, can you tell me a little more about your mother and her family? Was she a happy person?

(*Pause for twenty-three seconds—sounds of boiling water and the washing of dishes and cups*)

MOM: It's sad. Your grandmother's mom was old, so her aunt or sister raised her. They didn't come down to Seoul with her. I don't really know what happened. Her family was poor too, so she married at a young age, around eighteen, maybe younger.

CRYSTAL: To Grandfather?

MOM: Yes. There was eleven-year age difference between them, and Grandfather already had a family from his first marriage. Grandma was depressed and   . Every day, she cried so much. She felt so alone and Grandfather   .   her when they were young. They   . Whenever I remember that Grandmother was not happy, I think, *Oh, maybe that's why she got cancer or something.* She cried all the time. Even though I was young, I could feel it. When someone cries every day, those tears sink into you. So whenever I remember that Grandma was not happy, I wonder if this unhappiness is what made her sick. Sometimes I blamed my   . Maybe   , she wouldn't have been so sad, and the cancer wouldn't have been so bad. Or maybe marriage is just like that.

(*Water hissing as it boils in the pot*)

....

From an early age, I was depressed too, and sometimes, I felt like I didn't want to live anymore. Because I was not happy. Those two things are related, you know. If your mom is not happy, then the children are not happy either. And if you are not happy for a long time, it changes you.

In this recorded conversation where she describes being mothered and mothering her children through cooking, my mom lets her guard down and reveals two profound memories that have stuck. First, she describes her depression as a lifelong struggle and something she navigated *since her childhood days in Korea.* For most of my life, I assumed that my father was the primary culprit for Mom's melancholic tendencies. But in this half-hour span, Mom proves me wrong. She hints at other underlying factors. Relatedly, she describes how her sadness is connected to her own mother's struggle with depression, as if this affective connection is an umbilical cord that forever tethered her body to my grandmother's. *When someone cries every day, those tears sink into you.... Those two things are related.... If your mom is not happy, then the children are not happy either.*

These comments are brief but potent. My mother's description of my grandmother as a sorrowful person makes me wonder about the everyday conditions she navigated during the first half of the twentieth century. Learning more about this history could clarify the circumstances that contoured my grandmother's emotional interiority, and her relationships with her children and husband. In turn, these familial relationships modeled for my mother how to inhabit the world, and which parts of herself to show and which parts to hide. Unexpectedly, the cooking lesson alludes to the ways that my mother's life story is part of a diasporic family history mapped by violence, displacement, and survival. I imagine how these dynamics congealed over decades, sinking through my mother's porous skin and settling into the density of her bones, her muscle matter, and the synaptic thicket of nerve bundles.

....

My maternal grandmother's name was 허복남, or Huh Bok Nam (née). Locating details about Bok Nam's early life has not been an easy task. My memories of my grandmother are few and sparse because I was only eight when she passed away from her decade-long struggle with cancer. Before then, I intermittently saw her at family gatherings, like New Year's Day, when my sisters, cousins, and I visited my grandparents' home in Los Angeles. I remember Grandma as a warm and affable per-

son who always hugged her grandchildren as she tenderly brushed loose strands of hair from their faces. This sharply contrasted with my maternal grandfather, who was stoic in his black horn-rimmed glasses and rarely gave his children or grandchildren hugs. In these memories, my grandmother is standing in the background, observing her grandchildren as they chase each other in the spacious backyard. She is wearing elegant clothes in pale hues that fit gracefully around the soft curvature of her shoulders and hips. To my sisters and me, our grandmother is mesmerizingly beautiful. When Auntie Kyung and Mom wistfully reminiscence about her, they share how wonderful of a mother and wife she was. One of the many lessons that Bok Nam shared with her daughters is that as women, they should never leave the bedroom without making themselves presentable to the outside world. Like my mother, my grandmother, I suspect, drew on her beauty as leverage to secure what she needed in a world that hadn't provided her with much comfort or ease, or many resources. At markets, she always received the best cuts of meat and vegetables, and at school, she charmed her children's teachers with her quick wit and beauty.

Bok Nam was born on March 8, 1922, in the industrialized city of Hamhŭng in north Korea to a working-class family of the sangmin, or "commoner" class. Bok Nam's mother passed away when she was young, and her elderly father was, according to Auntie Kyung, a Christian minister, although my mother can't recall this detail. Born on June 13, 1911, near the fishing center of Riwŏn, roughly 160 kilometers away from Bok Nam's hometown, my maternal grandfather 김기운, or Kim Kiun, was born to a poor sangmin family of tenant farmers who worked the land for generations. I don't know very much about Riwŏn and Hamhŭng other than that both cities lie near South Hamgyŏng's eastern coastline, which touches the East Sea. Hamhŭng is now north Korea's second-largest city after P'yŏngyang and exists on an irregularly shaped plain adjacent to the Sŏngch'ŏn River, a sliver of water mentioned in the mythological origin stories of the Korean Peninsula.

Similarly to my father's family, my mother and her siblings share more details about their father than they do about their mother. Grandma never spoke about her family, whom she left in 1946 when she migrated to Seoul with my grandfather, his mother, and their four children, including three stepchildren and Auntie Insuk. Mom and her siblings describe their father as an ornery but intelligent man who navigated extreme poverty to become a medical doctor. By the time he was ten years old, his father passed away, and as the eldest son, Kiun became financially responsible for his mother and siblings. My grandfather was bullied by his classmates for wearing clothes that frayed at the seams. But rather than subject himself to this ridicule, he dropped out of school in the third grade, dedicating himself to self-study when he was not working. Every day before and after work, he read books he'd borrow from his employer, a doctor, who became a mentor for the next two decades. Years later, my grandfather became one of the few people in south Korea to pass the national medical board exam without a formal education. Kiun was married once before he met my grandmother. When he was in his late twenties, his first wife died, leaving him with three young children to care for, including a child disabled by an unknown illness when he was a baby.

I am struck by this pattern of silence and silencing affixed to my grandmothers' lives on both sides of my family. By and large, my grandmothers' experiences are overshadowed by the success of their professionally accomplished husbands. I know my grandmothers' names and what they looked like, but the tone of their voices and their preferences, fears, and desires are occluded from the family memory archive. These notable absences are not just erasures but also a directive: They tell generations of my family who to remember and who to forget. Out of frustration but also determined love, I fill the expanse of these pages with my maternal grandmother's presence; she exerted extraordinary influence on my mother's life. Alongside these gaps and uncertainties, I tell her that she has *always* been here.

....

Often, Confucianist ideology is assumed to be the global cause of Korean women's misery because of its patriarchal, classist, and sexist assumptions. But it is only one factor out of many that shaped my maternal grandmother's social world. In the first half of the twentieth century, conditions in her life were rapidly changing. Confucian ideals of filial obligation, women's expected obedience to men, and gendered and class-based hierarchies were reaffirmed as much as they were challenged, resisted, and reformed against the backdrop of Japanese colonization. My grandmother's world morphed again after the fall of Japanese rule, which coincided with the military occupation of Korea by other colonial forces, and a catastrophic war.

Bok Nam came into young adulthood in the late 1930s. This was during the period of late Japanese imperialism, where the colonial regime tightened its grip on cultural assimilation by banning the use of the Korean language in schools and other public places.[5] Cultural discourses on women's labor were also changing.[6] While colonial governance emphasized that Korean women's "proper" place was in the home, there were competing philosophies that provided texture to these ideals. Nationalist ideology, infused with Western scientific ideals regarding "professional housewifery" and the Korean discourse of the "New Woman," challenged neo-Confucianist norms that relegated women *solely* to the family home. Korean women's labor contributions to the national economy were increasingly embraced, if such work did not hinder women from fulfilling their duties as good daughters, wives, and mothers.[7] Of course these ideals were primarily concerned with women of the yangban, or the ruling and gentry class. Poor and working-class women in Korea, like my grandmother, had always worked out of necessity: They were perceived as outside of the realm of ideal womanhood because they were forced to work outside of the home for their family's survival. Still, the industrial development of Korea under Japanese colonial rule placed more and more women, including those who were educated, into the labor force. By the end of the 1930s, tenants, agricultural wage workers, and industrial laborers constituted more than three-quarters of the total Korean population.[8]

In May 1938, the Japanese colonial government instituted the National General Mobilization Law, which established programs for war mobilization in Japan and its colonies, including Korea. The National Registration System, issued in December 1941, mandated that all Korean men and women between the ages of twelve and forty register with the government for enlistment in war-related services. Under these ordinances, the Women's Labor Volunteer Corps was established to recruit poor, uneducated, and unskilled Korean women for food processing mills and textile and rubber factories in Korea and Japan.[9] Thousands of unmarried women were also forced into sexual slavery as "comfort women" for the Japanese Imperial Army. Taken from their homes under false premises, nearly 150,000 Korean women were stationed at barracks and near battlegrounds across Japan, Okinawa, China, the Philippines, Burma, Thailand, and Indonesia.

I offer this tumultuous overview of the world that Bok Nam was a part of because it likely played a role in my grandmother's marriage to my grandfather. How could it not have? When my grandparents were introduced to each other through a matchmaker, my grandmother was in her late teens or early twenties, which places their arranged marriage between the late 1930s and early 1940s. This moment aligns with Japan's mobilization of a wartime colonial workforce, and the tightening of cultural regulations and state surveillance. While most Koreans were recruited for wartime labor, colonial ordinances permitted an exception for women: married status. Only unmarried women were required to enroll for imperial service.[10] Following her wedding day, my grandmother never worked outside of the home.

Perhaps Bok Nam married Kiun because her family feared she would be recruited for overseas colonial labor in and beyond Japan; or maybe they felt as if marriage would provide a modicum of safety against the terrifying claws of colonial surveillance. Whatever the reason, I wonder whether my grandmother was relieved with this arranged marriage to a lonely widower eleven years her senior. Or did she feel trapped, as if she was choosing between a rock and a hard place? When I consider the historical circumstances that led to her arranged marriage, I sense that Bok Nam desired a life where she could determine her own fate; or maybe I am projecting my own wishes onto my grandmother.

This tumultuous time was also the moment when my grandmother's sadness was sown.

Though I know little about my grandparents' marriage, I sense that the first decades of their relationship were arduous. Overnight, a young Bok Nam became a mother to three stepchildren; between 1944 and 1955, my grandmother bore six other children. Despite having interests in music, reading, and dance, child-rearing kept Bok Nam busy. As Mom puts it, my grandmother was bright and had a curiosity that couldn't be easily tamed. But she was dependent on my grandfather, relying on him for food, shelter, clothing, and other necessities. While my grandfather was a devoted father who fiercely advocated for his children's education—especially for his daughters, which was unusual at this time—he was not an emotionally effusive person. When I ask Uncle Sukjin about this aloofness, he gently shares that his father suffered his own childhood wounds that impacted how he expressed love. *Your grandpa provided for everyone, and that was how he loved people.* Still, I wonder about my grandmother's relationship with Grandpa, and whether she longed for emotional warmth, tenderness, and affection from her husband as a young spouse. During those early years, Kiun also made it clear to Bok Nam that her place was in the home. At some point, an aunt remembers my grandmother sitting at the kitchen table thumbing through a newspaper. When my grandfather saw this, he took the paper away from her, inquiring how she could possibly have time to read when she had children to rear and care for. When I tentatively asked my mother about this, she couldn't recall ever seeing my grandmother read a newspaper or book during her childhood.

Alongside these dynamics that potentially ushered Bok Nam into a marriage she felt unprepared for, my grandmother was one of millions of people separated from her family and kin during the Korean War. By autumn 1945, Korea was divided into northern and southern halves. Due to financial instability, my grandparents relocated to Seoul in 1946, where others from their respective hometowns had already resettled.[11] With almost nothing in their possession, Bok Nam and Kiun migrated to Seoul with their growing family in tow, which at that point included four children and my grandfather's mother. At some point, Grandfather's brother and nephew traveled to Seoul, but this brother crossed back into the north for political reasons, leaving his only son in the hands of his uncle. As my grandparents experienced alongside hundreds of thousands of other Koreans, having wŏlbuk gajok in their genealogical line, or a family member who voluntarily crossed to the north, was stigmatizing if not dangerous.[12] When my grandparents were preparing to move to the United States in 1974, my grandfather was called into a cramped Korean Central Intelligence Agency (KCIA) office where he was questioned for hours about his "traitor" brother in north Korea.[13] During the hours-long interrogation, my grandfather learned what became of his brother: Officials informed him that his brother had become a prominent police chief and member of the Workers' Party of Korea. When I ask Auntie Kyung and Uncle Sukjin about my grandmother's side of the family, they tell me that everyone, besides a single cousin, remained in the north. After 1946, Bok Nam never saw her family again during her lifetime.

Scholars of Korean studies like Nan Kim and Heonik Kwon have written about the profoundly personal implications of the Korean War.[14] The intimacies of kinship are at the heart of the Korean War, not only because so many families were separated or because bloodlines were weaponized by the south Korean government to punish families it considered leftist provocateurs.[15] In addition, the meaning of family shifted after 1950 due to south Korea's rapid urbanization and north Korea's revolutionary social transformation.[16] These processes led to narrower constructions of family. Before these changes, family had encompassed more elastic understandings that sutured gajok (the nuclear family) to ilga (communities associated with a specific place or location). In this more expansive expression, people unrelated by blood referred to each other as "brother" and "sister," as well as "cousin," "uncle," and "aunt." This capacious articulation makes me curious about the wider circle of people my grandmother left behind beyond her family of origin, including neighbors, friends, and schoolmates.

When I have asked Mom about whether Grandmother ever spoke of this separation, she provides the same response in a flat tone: Bok Nam never mentioned this experience to her. But Mom still mentions to me how Grandma, throughout her life, seesawed between episodes of inconsolable sadness and volcanic anger. There were days when she would cry for hours without disclosing the reason for her tears. In considering these circumstances, I imagine how devastating these losses must have been for Bok Nam. To experience the cruelty of indefinite family separation, especially during a time of total war, is to confront a frightening futility: No matter how much one begs, cries, and screams at the horrendous injustice, those in positions of power rarely listen. For them, war—and, relatedly, death—is a lucrative enterprise and a ripe solution for stealing and securing what never belonged to them.

During these moments when Bok Nam is alone with her memories, I see my grandmother sitting on her bed as she remembers her favorite sister. The passage of time has not changed her older sister's appearance: Frozen in time, she still has the same beautiful elfish face with its deep dimples and expansive smile. Staring down at her weathered hands, Bok Nam wonders whether she will ever see her beloveds again after decades of separation. *Would I greet my sister as a familiar or stranger?* Suddenly, she trembles as nausea radiates from her body's core to the back of her throat. Even after division, the short distance wedged between my grandmother and her family allows her to sense their shared sorrow across the border. Hamhŭng is 171 miles from Seoul, less than the distance between Los Angeles and San Luis Obispo, a two-and-a-half-hour car ride. This scenario is maddening to think about, even though millions of people live and die with such a reality.

My grandmother's silence isn't an anomaly or exceptional; among survivors of war and catastrophe, it is exceedingly common. At an academic conference, a friend and scholar of critical refugee studies once told me, *No one wants to speak about something that could destroy them.* But silence is slippery and multifaceted. It can simultaneously reflect a determination to quietly rebel and protest. In her posthumously published memoir, *Landbridge: Life in Fragments*, Y-Dang Troeung intimates this when she shares the Khmer proverb dam-doeun-kor, or "to plant a kapok tree."[17] To Cambodians, the kapok tree is significant because its quiet, rooted presence during their country's genocide symbolized how everyday people survived this terrifying stretch of time: Within a ravaged landscape, silence provided groundcover for buried roots so that a future could still be possible. In this way, my grandmother's silence was indicative of her will and desire to survive. Her silence also demonstrated how her sorrow was dismissed as a secondary concern unworthy of acknowledgment and attention. During this cooking lesson, Mom repeatedly mentions how heartbroken Bok Nam was, so much so that Mom identifies my grandmother's internalized sadness as the origin of her death.[18]

Both of my maternal grandparents passed away from terminal illnesses—my grandmother from multiple myeloma in 1988, and my grandfather from an aggressive form of prostate cancer in 1996. While Bok Nam lay dying, my mother spent long hours sitting by my grandmother's bedside as a caregiver, first at my grandparents' home and then at the hospital. Though I was too young to remember every detail of my grandmother's decline, I can still recall the shock I felt when I saw how much she had transformed within a few months. As the cancer furiously consumed Grandma's body from the inside out, she became thinner and weaker, losing all her hair, while her skin transformed into a translucent gray. During the last weeks of her life, Grandma mumbled names during her sleep as my mother held her hand. Though she listened attentively, my mother didn't recognize any of these whispered words. My grandmother must have been dreaming about her family in Hamhŭng, preparing to meet them following a lifetime of separation.

....

Despite these struggles, my grandmother was not a passive bystander in life. Bok Nam, like other working-class women, was tough as nails, and at times, she pushed against social expectations. Sometimes, this pushing back was intentional, and other times, it was necessary for survival. This is evident in the handful of stories that Auntie Kyung shares with me. She speaks to my grandmother's survival instincts and her ability to think quickly on her feet.

In one such story, Auntie Kyung describes how her parents left north Korea in 1946. While traveling south to Seoul with his family, my grandfather became anxious over the slow pace of travel and took off on his own, telling his wife and mother that he would travel to Seoul first to secure safe housing. During this time, my grandmother was two months pregnant with Auntie Kyung and responsible for caring for and protecting four children and her mother-in-law. Somehow, she safely guided her family to Seoul, eluding US military inspections and DDT delousing stations, which became more common along the 38th parallel and at crowded train stations where refugees from the north disembarked. From accounts that document people's harrowing journeys across the north-south border before its closure, most refugees traveled on foot for miles before being loaded into packed train cars.[19] I imagine Bok Nam crossing the mountainous terrain and thick forests along the border, with her small children and mother-in-law trusting her to guide them to safety. When I envision this dangerous journey with all of its unknowns, my face flushes with heat. I am frustrated with, even angry at, my grandfather for leaving my grandmother with this staggering responsibility. But maybe Bok Nam had already become accustomed to navigating harrowing challenges within her family.

Another story: In January 1951, the People's Volunteer Army of China and north Korean forces recaptured Seoul for the second time during one of the most brutal periods of fighting, which US historians refer to as the Third Offensive. During this chaotic time, thousands of northern migrants in Seoul, including my grandparents, moved further south in search of refuge. Their decision to leave Seoul was hasty because it was sparked by the south Korean military's sudden visit to their home in the middle of the night in their search for doctors. As Stephen Hong Sohn writes about his own family in *Minor Salvage: The Korean War and Korean American Life Writings*, these visits by the anticommunist military and police officers were common during the war in south Korea.[20] Sometimes, they were used as a fear tactic and, other times, as a surveillance tool to weed out communist sympathizers. As my grandfather hid and surreptitiously listened from a crawl space, an officer pointed a gun at my grandmother's head, demanding the whereabouts of her husband. My grandmother didn't hesitate and told him exactly where my grandfather was hiding. While I'm surprised to hear this and laugh from shock, Auntie Kyung shares that my grandmother's disclosure was not a betrayal but rather a practical split-second decision: Although she feared that her children would die without her, she knew she would survive without her husband.[21]

Immediately after this incident, my grandparents and their family fled Seoul and migrated 127 kilometers south to Yesan County. Once again, my grandfather left on his own, though he secured a truck to take his wife, mother, and now five children to Yesan.[22] During this long journey south, my grandmother was eight months pregnant with my mother; later, she gave birth to her in Yesan on February 17, 1951. In 1953, after the signing of the Korean armistice, my grandmother finally returned home to Seoul with her children and mother-in-law without Grandpa. During the grueling two-week journey, she crossed the unpredictable currents of the Han River and found shelter for her family. After sharing these tales of escape and return, Auntie Kyung sighs. *I don't know how my mother did it, but she is the reason we survived.*

....

From the Archival Hold: The Hamhŭng Friends

There is an archive of family photographs I inherited from my mother's family. I am especially drawn to a batch of older images that are nearly a century old. Since my grandparents were continuously displaced

throughout the 1940s and 1950s, I am in awe of how they managed to carry these photos with them across bullet-pocked bridges and a mountainous terrain littered with hidden mines. As I hold these fragile photographs in my hands, I feel immense gratitude that my grandparents survived the war and displacement and that they were able to preserve these images for their grandchildren to touch and see.

In one image, a young Bok Nam is photographed with a group of handsome women. This portrait is weathered and torn at the right edge, erasing two figures from the top row. My grandmother is featured in the second row, third from the left, and is wearing a hanbok with a long-sleeved wrap top and full-length skirt. Her hair is elegantly styled, and she stares directly at the camera with hands neatly folded over her lap. Nearly all these women are intently staring at the camera with focused expressions. While the photograph looks staged, I feel a warm camaraderie among the group. Several women in the back row are lightly touching each other's shoulders, while women in the front row are kneeling with their draped skirts brushing against each other. When I show this image to a close friend, she comments on how sturdy these women look. I nod in agreement.

Similarly to most of these family photographs, there is no name, date, or location that accompanies this image. By how young she looks, my educated guess is that this portrait was taken while Bok Nam was in her late teens (seventeen or eighteen?), which dates the photograph to 1939 or 1940. While photography studios were still fledgling in Korea during the colonial period, there were several spaces that opened in urban centers like Seoul (known then as Keijō), P'yŏngyang (Heijō), and possibly Hamhŭng (Kankō). Social etiquette dictated separate photography studios for women so they could show their faces without the protective cover of long cloaks.[23]

What was the purpose of this gathering, and why document it with a studio portrait? In my dreams, I imagine that these women are Bok Nam's classmates and that they are marking their last day of school together. Or maybe they are close friends who visited a P'yŏngyang portrait studio to celebrate the crispness of spring. When I close my eyes, I can see and hear Bok Nam giddily holding her breath, tilting her head back in laughter as she rides the tram for the first time. P'yŏngyang's central boulevard is lined with the fluttering petals of cherry blossoms, with pedestrians and bicyclers navigating the busy buzz of midday traffic. Other times, I fantasize that these women belonged to a secret theater society, stealthily led by Bok Nam, who developed a flair for the dramatic and an adoration for draped costumes and voluminous hats. Just beyond this photograph's borders, Bok Nam plots her next move beyond the conventions of marriage. This photograph is a memento from Bok Nam's *other* life, in which she refuses to enter an arranged marriage and instead continues her education at the university. She remains close to the theater, becoming a prominent playwright and essayist—which, for a woman of working-class roots, was unheard of at this time. Through the magic pull of writing, she inhabits her body with a contentment she has never felt before. Over the next decade, Bok Nam builds a robust intellectual life in P'yŏngyang, connecting with a vibrant circle of writers, actors, artists, and scholars who encourage her to write. But life can change in an instant. Beginning in the summer of 1950, United Nations–approved bombs obliterated nearly every building, school, theater, Buddhist temple, and hospital in P'yŏngyang. Following the disappearance of her older sister and father, she flees south with a cadre of other writers. Bok Nam is separated from her city, without knowing if she will ever return.

Decades later, as she smokes a cigarette and gazes at the Han River from her apartment in Seoul, she daydreams of the P'yŏngyang of her youth. In a new play she is writing, *The Hamhŭng Friends*, there is a scene that features a young woman and her school friends as they visit a photography studio for a group portrait. The playwright describes how this photograph marks a turning point: It is a day before these friends scatter to other parts of Korea, Manchuria, and the Japanese metropole as wartime colonial laborers. While no one speaks, there is a nervous energy that percolates in the studio as these women anticipate what life holds for them. Life can change in an instant. Bok Nam asks, *What unfolded for these friends after this photograph*?

Staring at my grandmother's youthful face in this photograph, I realize that no one else knows of Bok Nam's other life except for me. Through this vision she shared with me, she imagines a future that had not yet arrived for her.

....

As I write about Bok Nam and my mother, it is impossible to locate, with precision, the origins of Mom's depression. Instead, by sitting with Bok Nam and what could have been, I am beginning to understand my mother's sadness as a medium of relationship building; her sorrow is integral to how I have come to know and relate to her. Relatedly, my grandmother's depression was the primary means through which my mother came to know and understand Bok Nam, so much so that she perceived her mother's desolation as her own. *Those two things are related, you know. If your mom is not happy, then the children are not happy either.*

In this way, I don't think of chronic depression as a fixed genetic inheritance but as one potent way to encounter and feel our family. When I speculate on the conditions that fostered my mother's depression, I think of Clara Han's poignant observations in *Seeing Like a Child: Inheriting the Korean War*. In her book, Han writes that children come to understand family as an experiential "scene of intimate relations" rather than as an "institution formed in advance."[24] In other words, the child *experiences* family through entwined relationships that are navigated, at times, for their own survival. In turn, familial relations introduce us to the world and our initial place in it. As the youngest girl in the family, my mother was repeatedly told to never complain and to be grateful for all she was given during a time of war and precarity. Through her own mother's silence, she learned that there were things she should never talk or ask about. When she transitioned into adulthood, she observed the ways that women were expected to take care of their spouses and children, even with disheartening costs. As such, descriptors like *war*, *family separation,* and *gender and class norms* never found a place in my mother's vernacular vocabulary. Instead, these categories permeated her life through the intimacy of interpersonal relations with family, friends, neighbors, teachers, classmates, and possible suitors.

When I reread the transcript of the cooking lesson with my mom, I consider whether my mother learned grief *and* survival from Bok Nam. I am also struck by the similarities between my mom's descriptions of her mother and the emotional fluctuations I experienced as a child. My mom's warmth was most palpable during the times she cooked for her daughters. No matter how busy she was, she packed us elaborate vegetable-and-fried-egg sandwiches for lunch and provided us with beautiful birthday meals replete with ddak-doritang, or spicy chicken stew, and rich buttercream-frosted cakes from our favorite Korean bakery in Garden Grove. During nights when I was restless and could not fall asleep, my mother would snuggle in bed with me, gently brushing my hair until my breathing slowed. These tender moments were punctured by unpredictable episodes of rage when my sisters and I didn't receive the grades she expected, or when my father failed to return home in the evening as promised. My mother's childhood exemplified for her the expectations, contradictions, and disappointments of parenthood and marriage. When my mother first became a young parent, these experiences provided a working blueprint for how to love and take care of my sisters and me.

Most of all, I wonder about the options available to my grandparents as they sought sanctuary from the instability and poverty they experienced after peninsular division. For nearly two decades after 1950, protecting and providing for their burgeoning family was their sole priority. There was no such thing as self-care in their lives; or if there was, it was cast aside as a frivolous luxury that only the wealthy could afford. I also contend with the stigmatization of disability and madness in postdivision Korea. During this time, there was an absence of nonpathologizing language that could hold the depth of the utter sorrow and destruction that millions of people experienced during a time of war and occupation. This absence preceded Korean division as well: Under Japanese colonial rule, the Korean nation was described by demoralized politicians, activists, and print media as disabled and feminized, which clearly demonstrates the existing ways that disability and femininity were perceived as markers of social inferiority.[25] But in a contradictory sense, women's bodies in Korea were also considered pivotal to the project of national preservation, whether as healthy mothers responsible for reproducing the family or as the moral linchpin of the family and nation. Consequently, those perceived as outside of these normative bounds—disabled, poor, infertile, depressed, mad, and so on—were defined as degenerative citizens in need of curative rehabilitation.

This characterization of disability makes me somber for my grandmother and mother. My grandmother lacked the language to name her depression as a symptom of social violence. Even if she had access to these words, she refrained from expressing her struggles with her husband and children, perhaps due to a fear of shaming or rejection. Following her marriage to my grandfather, she observed traces of these dynamics in her family. Sunsook, a child from my grandfather's first marriage, suffered a devastating illness as a baby that left him physically and cognitively disabled for the remainder of his life. In passing conversations, my mother shared with me that Sunsook didn't live with the rest of the family but in an adjacent house with her paternal grandmother, who took care of this grandson until he passed away. He is missing from all of the studio family portraits in my possession. When I inquired why this brother didn't live in the same house as the rest of the family, my mom mentions that her mother, as a new and young bride, was too inexperienced to care for so many children. Bok Nam must have felt overwhelmed by the prospect of raising three young children on her own. But very likely, Sunsook's disabilities were stigmatized by the larger society, with my grandfather shielding, even hiding, his son from the world. When I reminiscence on my mother's resistance to caring for her sadness and depression, I wonder whether this is a consequence of what she saw, heard, and experienced as a child.

....

In 1971, Uncle Sukjin and my mother traveled to the United States for an extended visit. When my mother shared this experience with me years ago, she described it as a leisurely break from college. By the time my mother was in high school, my grandfather's private medical practice and his ownership of land just north of Seoul had proven profitable. He could finally afford to send all his children to college and graduate school, not only in south Korea but also in the United States. As a beautiful person on the cusp of adulthood, my mom took a temporary leave from college to experience freedom elsewhere. Mom also missed her eldest sister, Insuk, whom she considered a second mother and who by that time had moved to the United States. She desired to see, firsthand, what her sister's life was like beyond her parents' vigilant gaze.

On all counts, the photographs I've seen from this time reaffirm this storyline. In Polaroids from 1971, my gorgeous mother is spending time at a beach with friends. Wearing a fashionable short red jumpsuit, with a breeze brushing against her shoulder-length black hair, she has a mischievous grin on her face. There is a caption written in Korean on the back of one of these photographs, which I've translated as *spending time with friends in the United States*. These Polaroids are time capsules: There is a faint glow to these snapshots, as if the sun's radiant rays have been embedded in the celluloid surface. My mother looks so lighthearted, and I wonder who she was at this special time of her life.

Recently, Uncle Sukjin and Auntie Kyung communicated varied stories affixed to these Polaroids. Their versions do not contradict what my mother shared. They simply add complexity to the storyline. My auntie shares that my mother experienced cyclic depression throughout childhood, as did several other siblings in the family. In the 1970s, she struggled with a depressive spell and took time off from college to accompany her younger brother Sukjin to the United States. Her family hoped that a new environment would lift her mood. This seemed to work for some time, but my mother's depression eventually returned in heightened form.

Uncle Sukjin shares that in 1971, my mother and he arrived in Chicago to visit family and explore university options in the United States. By that point, my grandfather's children from his first marriage were already in the States. My aunties Kyung and Youngsuk were preparing for medical residencies on the East Coast, while Insuk had moved to Chicago to begin a new life with her husband. The youngest son, Sukyoon, remained in Seoul. After a brief stay with Insuk, Uncle Sukjin and Mom moved to Baltimore, where they eventually took classes at the University of Maryland. But within several months, my mother was having trouble adjusting to life in the United States and returned to Seoul to finish school at Ewha Womans University. My uncle remained in Baltimore, later moving to Los Angeles, where my grandparents settled in 1974. My mother was one of the last ones in her family to leave Seoul. Though his words are vague, my uncle hints at this episode in our conversation. In a family timeline he quickly sketched for me during breakfast one morning, the caption under 1971 reads, *Later, Young Ok went back to Korea*.

....

A year ago, I scribbled the following in my journal:

> *It has been nine months or 39 weeks or 274 days since Dad passed away and Mom was taken away on an emergency hold.*

As recent as this history is, I have created an entombed anterior that can be described in the past tense. *This already happened; it's over now.* I am need of this temporal distance. The present as past, as done, as memory.

....

It is a Sunday afternoon in August 2023, and I am at my parents' house. Mom and I are seated next to each other at the kitchen table. As I fill her pillboxes for the next two weeks with a confetti of colorful medication, Mom is completing puzzles in a Sudoku book Coleen purchased for her. Even with the air conditioner on full blast, I feel uncomfortably warm as the late summer heat marinates the house. But while I wiggle in the chair with beads of sweat pooling behind my knees, Mom is perfectly focused on the task at hand. With her reading glasses perched on her nose and her white-haired head arched over the table, she is diligently completing each puzzle with numbers, square by square, with her neat handwriting. Occasionally, I interrupt her concentration by asking her how she is doing. She looks up with an inquisitive look, responding in a tired voice, *Fine*. Then her voice deepens as she begins to explain strategy to me. *Mun-hye-ya, you must make sure that you don't use the same number twice in the same row.* I nod while she works.

As time passes, I catch more glimpses of who my mother used to be. But also, she is a different person from the one I knew for the first forty-two years of my life. While she used to be the center of every public outing and family event we attended together, she now rarely steps outside by herself. Besides toasting slices of bread or warming up food that a hired caregiver has prepared, Mom stays away from the kitchen. As I'm sitting next to my mother, touching the cool softness of her arm, the question of writing about her life returns to me. *Do I have the right to share these stories about her?* I continue to struggle with this question. Yet, at the same time, I am uncertain whether it is possible to draw a definitive line between my parents' stories and my own. Over the years, their stories and silences have melded into my life, shaping me in the most habitual ways—from my tendency to overthink and overwork, to the difficulty of forgetting and forgiving, to a pervasive anxiety that colors how I approach the present and future. By sharing their stories, I am writing my own story.

At least for now, I allow this question to rest. It is dusk, and slanted cuts of pink-yellow light stream into the dining room through the window blinds. As Mom completes her Sudoku puzzles for the day, I am surprised by how much the expression on her face—the curved corners of her mouth, the earnest look in her eyes—resembles a photograph of her as an adolescent in Korea. In this black-and-white image, my mother, Young, is wearing a short-sleeved flower-patterned dress as she walks against a verdant backdrop of wild trees and shrubs. She looks sweetly tentative as she steps toward the photographer (Her mother? Her father? A sibling?). *Should I stay where I am or continue walking?*, this baby inquires. Sometimes, when I imagine my mother as a child in Korea, I visualize her holding this photograph in her tiny hands and marveling at how much she resembles her parents. With her index finger, Young traces the delicate features of her face, where she can see her mother's high cheekbones and gentle eyes, and the corners of her father's mouth. This younger version of my mother, this little girl with luminous eyes, smiles as she wonders who and where she will be when she reaches the age of her parents.

Toggling between the photograph of this sweet child of the past and my mother as she is now, I am amazed at how people can carry the same facial expressions for their entire lives, even if they transform into someone new.

waiting
for the high water, without
fear, together

THE DIASPORIC FAMILY ALBUM

from where in the image does it emanate?
—TINA CAMPT, *Image Matters*

DURING A NEW YEAR'S family gathering at a Chinese Korean restaurant in 2020, my Uncle Sukyoon gifted me a heavy cardboard box. *I think you'll enjoy looking at these*, he said with a subtle grin. Two months prior, I had lamented to my uncle that I felt saddened by how little I knew about our family. I longed for hints or traces that could tell me more about our history in Korea, especially before the 1953 armistice.

When I return home that evening, it is late, and I am sleepy from the long drive; but I am eager to sort through the box's contents. As I open the lid, I gasp, and my eyes widen; in the box, I see five large photograph albums with velvet or leather covers, each of a different size and color. I gingerly open the first album and notice that its opening page is filled with a pasted illustration of a lonely winter scene with bare trees, a clear blue sky, and fresh snow on the ground. Below the image is a date and phrase handwritten in jet-black ink: "1965.1.29: 영자 언니로부터" ("From Youngja's sister"). This name and date are unfamiliar to me.

I continue to thumb through the album filled with dozens of photographs—mostly black-and-white, a handful in color, and a few Polaroids—that likely span over a century. Somehow, Uncle Sukyoon, the youngest in my mother's family, had squirreled away these photographs (for how long?) and was now passing them on to me for safekeeping. Preserved in plastic sleeves and elegantly edged with black corners, these photographs depict my grandparents as youthful teenagers before they married. In one image, my grandfather is featured in a family portrait as a handsome teenager (he must have been thirteen or fourteen years of age?). He is wearing a crisp black suit with neatly slicked hair. Given his attire and the appearance of the two taller men standing next to him—the younger man is wearing circular-rimmed Windsor glasses, while the older figure wears an elegant, light-colored hanbok—I assume that this photograph depicts his employer's (a physician) family. There are other family studio portraits taken over the years that include my grandparents and their children, including my mother, and snapshots of ebullient outdoor celebrations, like festive weddings with dozens of people eating and drinking. There is also a photograph of my mother's graduation from high school; in that image, my mom is laughing as she receives a bundle of balloons and flowers from two of her sisters. But mostly, there are photographs of people and places who remain mysteries to me. When I inquire with Uncle Sukyoon and other relatives about who and what these photographs contain, I find out that everyone who could share more information, like my grandparents and my eldest auntie, Insuk, has passed away. These diasporic family albums thus mark a double loss: They shelter photographs of people who remain nameless, and loved ones who are now ancestors. They are shadow elements, rather than a reliable vessel, of memory.

Since so many of these photographs refuse to disclose the histories entombed within their borders, I consider how this amends the meaning of the diasporic family album.[1] Is a family album still a family album when its contents are unmoored from the memories that provide nostalgic heft in the first place? Do these images hold significance if they are unable to reveal the identities of people? While I am initially disappointed by this foreclosure, the enigma of these photographs makes it easier to turn away from the romanticized idea that they embody objective or intractable truths. On the contrary, they compel me to consider how erasure is always integral to the curation of the family photo album. That is, the family photo album is a work of fiction. The album's steward selects a constellation of moments, places, and people they consider worthy of preservation, while other bodies and moments are occluded, as if they never existed at all. The diasporic family photo album remembers as much as it forgets. Still, I gently flutter these photographs between my fingers, as if I am enticing them to shed their secrets to me.

When I consider my affective attachment to the diasporic family album, I initially turn to the writing of Tina Campt. In *Image Matters: Archive, Photography, and the African Diaspora in Europe*, Campt engages the photograph without limiting it to the parameters of visual evidence. Rather than defining the photograph as a supplement to a foregone past, Campt writes with the photograph as a speculative enactment.[2] The photograph gestures to what could or might have been, rather than something that definitively was. Viewers play an active role in constructing the photograph's meaning. We ruminate on the conditions, exchanges, and feelings that contour the photograph's body, from its heart-center to its border-edge. What is the image communicating to us right now and at this moment?

Like Campt, I choose to encounter these photographs in the present tense: They are happening to me *now* rather than disclosing a buried past. The emergent nature of these photographs foregrounds to me how these images constitute a material extension of my maternal grandparents. I am moved by this realization: In the most essential sense, these photographs *are* because my grandparents and their children, including my mother, persisted through the eruptive haze of colonial occupation, war, and migration. In turn, these images refuse to exist as inanimate objects stowed away in storage boxes. Rather, there is a warm, palpitating presence to them, as if an ancient thread binds our bodies to one another. These photographs are my kin and my relatives. Their existence, after all, indexes my own becoming in this world. The story of family survival thus becomes the most meaningful significance of the diasporic family photo album: These photographs are here, and I exist.

In the absence of verifiable knowledge, these photographs offer other routes of feeling and knowing. They conjure memory through intuition, touch, and sight. For example, I am unable to definitively name who this child is in this portrait, but when I look at how she poses in front of the camera, my eyes twitch because the gesture of her left hand against the chair-as-prop uncannily resembles my maternal grandmother's stance. In my memories of her, my grandma is always leaning in the background with her shoulder pressed against a wall. Suddenly, this photograph transforms into a portal: I see the silhouette of my grandmother in this young girl's stance, so I speak with her. *Who are you?* When I hold the image in my hands at this precise moment, this photograph of the unnamed girl becomes my maternal grandmother.

the curvature of the arm, the silhouette against the wall

If these photographs are happening *now*,

    What stories, rumors, mythologies are imagined from their bodies?

        In the face of obstinate forgetting, what *else* emerges?

When I first received these albums from Uncle Sukyoon, my initial impulse was to protect the photographs. For over a week, I diligently digitized the images, saving them as electronic files and arranging each album into Dropbox folders to share with my mother's family. I thought that they, too, would be awed by their existence. But when I emailed my uncles, aunties, cousins, and sisters the Dropbox link, only two of them immediately responded, and no one seemed particularly excited. Later, two cousins shared how much they appreciated my efforts. In hindsight, I realize that my aunties and uncles might have had ambivalent reactions to my efforts to preserve these photographs. When they look at these images of their past, disquieting memories might surface for them. Given the litany of secrets that have shaped connections—as well as fallouts—in my mother's family, I would not be surprised if these photographs remind my relatives of what they cannot say out loud, or bring to the surface moments they would rather forget.

Mostly, I wanted to preserve these photographs for descendants who might be curious about, or lonesome for, their ancestors. But even the eternity promised by digitization is deceptive. The digital cloud is not an ethereal realm immune to disappearance. Their existence is conditioned by hardware, data, and motivations reflective of power, surveillance, and transformation.[3] Preservation is also based on a premise, or rather a promise, that something will last forever. As the scholar-artist Latipa observes, this promise of forever is a dangerous invention of the colonial regime.[4] In her multimedia artwork *The Archive's Fold*, Latipa looks for the faces and bodies of her family, including her great-great-grandmother Latipa, in colonial government archives located in the Philippines and United States. With dedicated focus, the younger Latipa travels through time and space in search of the elder Latipa. The national archives in Manila and Washington, DC, however, include family photographs of a different order: the colonial family, constituted by the colonizer and colonized. In lieu of photographs of her family of origin, there are other images that demonstrate the intimate relationship between colonial violence and photography. There are images of white ethnographers, soldiers, and officers carefully documenting cadavers, hung bodies, and decimated villages. There are photographs of Filipinas recruited into exploitative labor, like factory embroidery work for the US government and military. These photographs attest to how colonial regimes draw on visual technologies, like photography, to hold captive those they wish to control as test specimens. These visual traces are organs of memory for the colonial regime.

Over the course of a century, these techniques have trickled all the way down to everyday use and practices of digital preservation. Scientists, archivists, museum workers, government officials, and professional photographers have perfected techniques of preservation to safeguard images for longevity. There is an avid desire for permanence, for a *forever*, in this place we live in. What might it mean, then, to refuse this inheritance by encountering the photograph as a body that *will* deteriorate and disappear? How does our relationship to the diasporic family photo album shift when we humbly recognize that the photograph, like our own fleshed bodies, is finite, fragile, and limited in its life span?

Acknowledging the mortality of the photograph, of course, does not evacuate its ability to prophesize emergent futures. When I stare at photographs of my maternal grandmother in Seoul throughout the 1960s, they portend the rapid development that would furiously consume and transform south Korea in the decades to come. There is one photograph I am especially intrigued by, though I am uncertain who took this photograph and why. In this image, my grandmother is walking on a bustling sidewalk; she is wearing a traditional hanbok with a dark-colored flower-patterned chima, or skirt, and a pale-colored jeogori, or long-sleeved top overlain with an embroidered vest. Her face is slightly tilted toward her left as she glances to the side, refusing to look directly at the camera. This frozen expression hints that my grandmother is distracted by something or someone. But most unexpectedly, she holds a leather briefcase in her left hand as she briskly walks along a street bordered by storefronts. This one detail is piercing and changes the photograph for me—or as Roland Barthes might say, the briefcase is the photograph's *punctum*.[5] Based on stories my mother shared with my sisters and me, I assumed that my grandmother rarely left her house, at least by herself. But in this photograph, my grandmother looks undeterred, strong, and determined; the briefcase also hints that she is sensing a burgeoning life beyond the daily grind of domestic tasks. Turning away from the photographer's gaze, my grandmother sees and feels the constant change that is transforming the world around her. This photograph of Bok Nam is a key: It materializes into a border-space through which a vanishing past opens into a yet-to-be future.

in the space between the before and after

Similar impressions surface when I look at Polaroids of my maternal grandparents in New York City and Washington, DC. In these photographs, taken in April 1972, Grandma and Grandpa are visiting their children living abroad in the United States. There is a pair of Polaroids that are especially notable because they are taken in front of the most blatant symbols of US empire: the Statue of Liberty and the Twin Towers of the World Trade Center.

I study my grandfather's weathered face as he stoically poses with my grandmother in a pin-striped tie and pressed coat. The statue of Libertas, figured in the distance, is squeezed between my grandparents. I squint hard at the photograph, attempting to make out the chiseled face of the Roman goddess of liberty before moving to my grandparents' facial expressions. My grandfather's skeptical look warns me of America's gilded promise of richness offered to migrants who arrived in the country after 1965, as my mother's family did. *Don't be fooled*, my grandfather cautions me. For a moment, I am startled by this faded image of the ill-fated Twin Towers, before their collapse in September 2001. Somehow, these ghost buildings seem to presage the fraught lives my mother and father would lead after their hopeful move to Los Angeles in 1984. Enamored by the promise of empire gold, they arrived in the United States with generous support from my mother's family but left with hollowed bones that had been emptied of their fat and marrow.

These photographs hold fortunes and mishaps that I cannot yet see; there are muted prophesies tucked away in the urban terrain, waiting to be fulfilled, deferred, or stymied in the years to come.

a horizon of desire, a sky of (mis)fortune

On the back of several of these photographs, there are handwritten notes. In one family portrait that features my mother, her parents, and six of her eight siblings, including a half brother, the following description in Korean is included in the back: *69-9-17 The day my sister left for America*. The note is likely referring to the day that my Auntie Insuk left for Illinois with her husband, my Uncle Joe, to begin a new life as a bride. While I am unable to definitively confirm the note's author, my guess is that the handwriting belongs to my Uncle Sukyoon. Although he is the youngest of his siblings, he dutifully serves as the family documentarian. During holiday dinners, New Year's Day gatherings, birthday celebrations, and weddings, Uncle Sukyoon is rarely seen without a camera in tow. In his reserved way, my uncle expertly circulates the room as if he is a fly on the wall. I wonder if he was like this as a child—absorbing his surroundings, first through his eyes and then through the lens of the camera. When he emailed my sisters and me photographs from our father's memorial service with a loving letter, I was immensely touched by his thoughtfulness. I didn't realize he had documented this moment for us. I feel a tender connection to my Uncle Sukyoon because he, too, is the youngest in the family (I was born five minutes after my twin sister); he has also chosen to take up the role of the memory keeper among his kin.

I remind myself to ask Uncle Sukyoon, the next time I see him, whether the scribbles on these photographs belong to him. But sometimes, such opportunities never arrive. On the morning of January 13, 2024, at the age of sixty-eight, my Uncle Sukyoon suddenly passed away from pancreatic cancer—a diagnosis that took all of us by surprise. In my favorite photograph of my uncle as a child, his faint smile is the same expression that was etched on his face when he gifted me the box of diasporic family photo albums.

the memory keeper who died too young

THE MEMORY KEEPER

Let us belong to our ghosts
and them to us.

GRIEF AND RETURN

제사 | JESA FOR DAD

I.

1. Crystal lights the incense.
2. Crystal pours soju into the shot glass to the brim and circulates it around the incense holder three times.
3. Crystal pours soju into the bowl with dirt in three precise pours. Places the shot glass back onto the altar.
4. Crystal bows twice in front of the altar.
5. Crystal and Dan bow twice together in front of the altar.

II.

1. Crystal places the rice and jjigae with chopsticks and spoon onto the altar.
2. Crystal and Dan kneel before the altar. Dan pours soju into the shot glass to the brim. Crystal places the shot glass back onto the altar by Dad's portrait. Crystal and Dan stand, take three steps back, and bow twice.
3. Crystal kneels and removes the shot glass from the altar; circulates the shot glass around the incense once; and pours the liquor into the bowl with dirt.
4. Crystal and Dan kneel before the altar; Dan pours soju into the shot glass to the brim; and Crystal places the shot glass back onto the altar by Dad's portrait. Crystal and Dan stand, take three steps back, and bow twice.
5. Crystal kneels and removes the shot glass from the altar; circulates the shot glass around the incense once; and pours the liquor into the bowl with dirt.
6. Crystal and Dan kneel before the altar; Dan pours soju into the shot glass only to 70 percent of its capacity. Crystal places the shot glass back onto the altar by Dad's portrait. Crystal and Dan stand, take three steps back, and bow twice.

7   Crystal places the spoon into the rice bowl with the concave part facing west. The chopsticks are placed onto one of the side dishes.

III.

1   Crystal and Dan kneel and sit in front of the altar with a five-minute silence.
2   Crystal places three spoons of the rice and soup into the bowl of water.
3   Crystal and Dan stand up, take three steps back, and bow twice.
4   Crystal opens all the windows and doors to the house for four hours.

....

The work of the memory keeper

> There is holding as there is letting go
> There is remembering as there is forgetting
> There are words as there is silence
> There is joy as there is grief
> There is shape as there is ambiguity
> There are cycles as there are breaks
> There is presence as there is absence
> There is birth as there is death
> There are openings as there are closures
> There is living as there is disappearance
> There is return

In Korean, there is an honorific phrase we use when someone passes away: 돌아가 셨다 (dol-a-ga syeotda), or "to return."[1] This phrase communicates how death is a passage and transition, rather than a definitive end point.

But to where and to whom are we returning?

Do we return to a time-space where birth
precedes and follows death?

Do we return to a continuum (a closed circle)
that is destined to repeat again?

In this movement of return, what remains, disappears, mutates?

What must the body offer as testimonial to be
recognized by beloveds who have already arrived?

Among the living, there are keepers of memory. In our work, we memory keepers hold at the center ethical relations with the living and the dead. We remember those who have transitioned as ancestors; we also understand there are things we will never know. After all, memory does not cradle only words, images, laughter, pleasure, voices, tastes, and touch. There are also silences, abandonments, and charred letters that cannot be pieced back together. To keep memory with tenderness is to remain with these losses, not as void but as an invitation to possibilities. Only then can remembering make way for reparative potentiality.

....

Several months following my father's death and mother's hospitalization, I began to feel more spaciousness to reflect on my grief. I realized how solitary and lonely mourning was as a process. Beyond conversations with my husband and a few confidantes, there was an absence of shared time and space to experience my grief in intentional rather than reactive ways. When I returned to work from a leave of absence, the sheer number of demands and deadlines that awaited gave me the distinct impression that my grace period for mourning had all but expired. My grief was superimposed onto a segmented timeline where my parents' lives were locked into a calamitous past while my sisters and I were expected to move on with our lives in the here and now.

But grieving is not a fleeting feeling that dissipates because we need or want it to. Although it can become easier to navigate with the passage of time, grief spills into the capillaries of our cellular makeup, shaping how we sense ourselves and negotiate our relations with others. Early on, when I was deepest in my grieving process, it was difficult for me to distinguish the past from the present and future because they bled into one other. I was haunted by flashbacks of my father's last week and continued to schedule his weekly dialysis appointments into my calendar. In hindsight, I realize that this adamant refusal to move on was indicative of an unspoken desire to reckon with and better understand the conditions that led to my father's death and mother's illness.

As part of my slow grieving process, it was helpful to speak with bereaved friends who had recently lost a parent, partner, or child. Several of them generously shared with me the ways they mourned for their loved ones by caring for and stewarding their memories. Among Korean friends, ancestral funerary rituals known as 제사, or jesa, provided a conduit to channel their grief and loss in communal ways. Performed every year on the anniversary of a family member's death, jesa includes the offering of food and drink, incense, and prayers for ancestors. An altar is filled with the ancestor's portrait and their favorite foods, like rice, panch'an (side dishes), fruits, rice cakes, and libations. The family gathers in front of the altar and moves through an elaborate sequence of steps to honor their ancestor, including the lighting of incense, multiple rounds of bowing, and the burning of paper with the name of the deceased. There is something comforting about the cyclic nature of jesa. The living nurture a different relationship with our dead, not only as family, but also as ancestors. We hold communion with our ancestral kin through the warmth of ritual, food, and the presence of others. Year after year, the somatic repetition of movement—forehead and hands meeting the earth, as resinous incense permeates the room—produces muscle memory that becomes a part of the body.

From friends and through research, I learned that one of the most endearing intentions of jesa is to fortify relations between the living and the dead. This takes special resonance in contexts where people lose their lives in mass-scale catastrophes like war, occupation, and forced displacement. In Korea, ancestral rituals like jesa and other funerary processions have become potent political tools that vocalize the suppressed stories of the disappeared.[2] For instance, ancestral rituals provide survivors of the Korean War with opportunities to denounce the fatal atrocities committed against their loved ones. Conversely, these rituals create a time and space distinct from the everyday, as the dead and living are able to dwell together. In this othered realm, the dead find ways to express their anger and sorrow at their unjust deaths. They also offer love to family and friends who struggled for the exoneration of the deceased. In *After the Korean War: An Intimate History*, Heonik Kwon provides a touching example, that of Lee Won-sik and his wife, both murdered by the south Korean state and its ancillary forces.[3] Lee, an herbal medicine practitioner, was sentenced to death by the government in 1961 for organizing a bereaved families' rally on the behalf of those killed by anticommunist forces in Kanghwa Island in 1950, including his wife. In 2011, Lee was posthumously vindicated by a court in Seoul, which cleared him of all wrongdoing. Following this decision, the couple's children held their parents' jesa, and toward the end of the ceremony, the brother and sister stared in disbelief at the altar: Two spoons placed into separate bowls of rice intended for each parent gravitated toward one other, halting only after the handle tips gently touched each other.[4]

When I was struggling to feel my grief without being undone by it, I was moved and consoled by these ancestor rituals and mourning rites. The idea that these knowledges had existed for millennia and were harnessed by Koreans in different ways made me feel less alone in my grief. These rituals also offer another access point to my family history: They situate my father within a lineage in which the living are connected to, rather than severed from, our dead. Understood in this way, ancestry becomes an imaginative form of storytelling that cobbles together, however incompletely, the myriad ways in which our kin entered, inhabited, and left this world. It is through this lens that I greet my father differently: His becoming and ending were paved by violence cast across a century, including colonialism, war, abandonment, and division. In a parallel sense, I felt in need of a space that could hold a knotted grief that had begun to fall apart. Along one frayed thread, I felt heartbreak over the loss of my parents as I knew them. Along another, I bitterly thought about the irony of how I had become a citizen of the very country that had played such a crucial role in ripping apart my family in Korea.

This latter point is especially disturbing to me, given that so many Koreans I know still speak about their fidelity and gratitude to the United States for "saving" them from the "evils" of north Korean communism. I am reminded of a prayer offered several years ago by an elder during a holiday gathering: *Dear Jesus, we are thankful for this wonderful and abundant life in the United States.* In response, I mumble to myself, *Yes, we are here because you were there.*[5] When I attempt to make sense of the delusional ways in which the US state frames its catastrophic military exploits as benevolent democratic missions, I turn to the work of Mimi Thi Nguyen, who writes about the ways in which refugees in the United States are bound to a life of indebtedness. As a consequence of US-led wars in Southeast Asia during the second half of the twentieth century, millions of Vietnamese people were killed, maimed, orphaned, and displaced. Hundreds of thousands of others became refugees and were eventually resettled in the belly of the imperial beast—the United States.[6] In exchange for these passages, refugees are expected to express unabashed love, gratitude, and loyalty toward their new country and home. However, this "gift" of American resettled life is tantamount to a punishing debt, given that the only collateral accepted by the US state is social death, characterized by carceral surveillance, financial precarity, isolation, and illness.

But given that definitive closure over these matters seemed impossible, I wondered what *else* I desired beyond an emotional reckoning with what had befallen my parents. Where does my grief come from, and where will mourning take me?

....

RETURN

Intransitive verb: to go back or come back again; to go back in thought, practice, or condition.

Transitive verb: to give (something, such as an official account) to a superior; to bring, send to, or put back in a former or proper place; to restore to a former or to a normal state; to bring in (profit); to give back to the owner; to give or perform in return; to hit back.

Noun: the act of coming back to or from a place or condition; something given in repayment or reciprocation; an answering play.[7]

In her 2009 film essay, *Faces of Seoul*, Gina Kim returns to her birthplace of Seoul following an extended time away. In the film, Kim uses her camcorder to visit places that were once familiar, including an old subway station on Seoul's No. 1 Line; Namsan, or Nam Mountain, a tourist attraction that once housed a Shintō shrine during the Japanese colonial era; a night market; and a colonial prison rehabilitated into a historical museum. When she encounters these spaces with her camera, a disorienting dissonance emerges between Kim's childhood memories and what she experiences as an adult. Subway stations are dilapidated or have been renamed. Buildings, parks, and homes have been demolished and no longer exist. The rapid rate at which Seoul changes through erasure, reconstruction, and recalibration is breathtaking. The title of the film suggests the multiplicity of Seoul and the disjuncture that Kim experiences: What was once familiar has become strange. Kim observes, "What does 'here' mean when I say it? It surely refers to the location itself, the geographical latitude and longitude of the land. But it also means everything that lies above the ground. So if everything above the ground changes, can you still say it is the same place?"[8]

I take Kim's questions to heart when I remember my first trip back to Korea after a thirty-one-year absence. I left in 1984 and returned in 2015. In this first trip back, I was bewildered by the familiarity of certain sights, smells, and tastes. Even after three decades of separation, I recognized the ubiquitous sound of Korean *everywhere.* I felt comforted by the liquid heat of Seoul's humidity during Korea's monsoon season. The chirping sounds of the maemi, or cicadas, at dusk reminded me of my mother's voice when she read to me at night. The delectably crunchy bites of pat bingsoo, a shaved-ice dessert topped with red bean, fruit, and condensed milk, tasted like summer. After several days in Seoul, the density of the muscles and tendons in my body loosened, and my Korean returned to me with more ease. But in other ways, Seoul felt unknown to me, as if I was a stranger slipping into a home without permission. While I was only four when I left, I can still remember how small our neighborhood felt. There was the cozy jimjibang, or Korean sauna, my sisters and I frequented with my mother and our nanny, Sunja. There were family friends who lived across the street. I can faintly recall a nearby school and park. Now, all these places were gone, replaced by flashy restaurants with English signs, hip boutiques, shiny department stores, and the blinding lure of neon lights. The Seoul I knew as a child was long gone. My body felt out of time, out of place. *If everything above the ground changes, can you still say it is the same place*?

Perhaps, *return* isn't the word I should be using to describe this first trip. *To return* connotes that one is reverting to a familiar place or condition. *Return* becomes a naturalized synonym for *home*. The act of com-

ing back to or from a place or condition. But to where, to whom, and to what was I returning?

For my parents' families, Seoul was a haven, not by choice but by the violence of war. Both my maternal and paternal families were uprooted from northern Korea during the first half of the twentieth century, before I was born. Likely, I will never be able to return to the farmlands and cities where they were raised in North Pyŏng'an and South Hamgyŏng. Even if I were to visit, these places would have transformed so utterly that I am uncertain whether I would experience the land, mountains, and rivulets in similar ways to how my grandparents and great-grandparents experienced them.

How does this unended history of division disorient the ways we come to understand *return* in proximity to, or distance from, "home"? Is this land in the north my ancestor? If so, what happens when a family, people, or community are forever displaced from their ancestor-land? Does the longing for return eventually diminish or disappear, or does it transmute into disruptive dreams that vex our assumptions of home, family, and safety? What were my father's and mother's relationships to this severance, and how did they feel their divided families in their bodies?

....

In encountering my father as an ancestor, I reflected on the historical, political, and social conditions that formed the peaks and valleys of his life. While aspects of his trajectory are unique, the overarching themes of secrecy, estrangement, and displacement are starkly familiar because Korean friends have observed similar challenges in their own reckoning with muted family histories. As an affective compass, my grief points to the location of my father's life within a vast diasporic geography in which millions of other Koreans are also enmeshed. My father's death, then, is not a loss to get over but rather a rupture that has birthed ways to feel and put into language the contours of diasporic grief beyond a bounded "I" or "me."

This understanding of diasporic grief as a return to the communal rather than an individual psychic affliction is something I have learned from my training as a feminist scholar. The wisdom of women of color's writing, queer of color critique, and feminist disability studies, in particular, has taught me that grieving can be a reparative, even liberatory, process when it is intentionally rooted in an ethic of radical care for others and oneself. If we understand radical care as crucial yet "underappreciated strategies for enduring precarious worlds," grieving transforms into a synergistic process that acknowledges how premature death, suffering, and loss are not natural but are disproportionately experienced by bodies deemed disposable, even ungrievable, by the state.[9]

In her experimental writing, the performance studies scholar Sandra Ruiz speaks to the ligatures that bind radical care to grieving through a concept she theorizes as grief-work.[10] Ruiz understands grief-work as one way to care for and to be in solidarity with the deceased. In essence, grief-work reckons with how bodies marked as other, nonhuman, or subhuman have had to endure the fatal weight of annihilating violence, which includes "state violence, unnatural disasters, deadly viral strains, police brutality, colonial logics, and anti-Black violence."[11] Yet rather than solely focusing on loss and violence, Ruiz observes how the material and immaterial dimensions of grief-work—feeling, naming, and organizing against systems of institutionalized brutality—are foundational to the ethical ways we feel and inhabit the everyday. Grief-work encompasses how the living remember the dead by laboring toward a different world liberated from violence and harm.[12]

This underscores for me how grieving in militarized and occupied contexts is connected to shared grievance, or the right to name and protest systemic injustice. To articulate a grievance is to put into words the loss and pain experienced by a body, people, and/or community, with the adamant hope that the underlying causes of suffering are eradicated. In situations where institutions like the prison or university commit violence against civilians and workers, the powerful conveniently frame grievances as frivolous complaints made without merit.[13] But to have the courage to move through a grievance process, or to communicate a wrongdoing; to name who and what has caused harm; and to insist on justice, cessation, and repair demonstrates that the powerful cannot take away everything. While this work is not without its significant challenges, it encourages us to enact the world we want to live in. Grief-work in this way opens us to reparative potentialities that are revitalizing, as much as it is informed by rage and sorrow.

These observations may seem detached from my father. But the mutuality between grief and grievance in relation to Korea, family, and diaspora is profound because I can situate, with purpose, my father's life beyond the personal. Inki Baik was not only my father. He was a survivor of the Korean War. He was the son of migrants displaced from north Korea and was raised in a militarized colonial milieu in which anticommunism, familial separation, and social death were everyday realities. When he migrated to the United States, he became a stranger in a settler country that was never created for him. Mourning for Inki Baik as an ancestor, and, by extension, as a subject of history, brings into sharper relief the destructive violence that impacted how he lived and died.

Naming the intimacies that conjoin grief to grievance acknowledges the volatility and precarity my father felt, witnessed, and experienced as a child and an adult. Just as important, this conjuring contributes to a long process of undoing the entangled pain, harm, and estrangement gnarled within my ancestral communities.

....

In the Korean Peninsula, Jeju-do (Jeju Island), and the diaspora, shamanic cosmologies of ancestral grieving, mourning, and spiritual mediation are referred to as 무교 (Mugyo), or Mu-ism. Mu-ism encompasses shamanic divinations, rituals, and practices and has played a crucial role in the expressive culture of grief and mourning in Korea. Mu-ism is distinct from family veneration practices like jesa since its syncretic roots are not in Confucianism but in indigenous animism and deity worship. It has no central doctrine and is orally transmitted, with lines of continuity often, though not always, within a single family. In Mu-ism, the mudang, or shaman, mediates encounters with the dead and holds rites of spiritual purification, forgiveness, and healing.

From my readings of Mu-ism, it is clear how ancestral cosmologies have significantly shaped protest culture and political remembrance against the tragedies of peninsular division, war, and colonial and state violence throughout Korea's troubling history. For example, as others and I have written elsewhere, Jeju-do experienced a devastating history under the strangling rule of multiple regimes in the twentieth century, including Japanese colonial governance, US military occupation, and south Korean dictatorial rule.[14] Between April 1948 and 1955, between 10 and 33 percent of the island's population was killed, largely due to south Korean military and ancillary counterinsurgency activities that crushed civilian protests against US occupation and division. Now referred to as the 4.3 (or April 3rd) Incident, Uprising, or Massacre, this brutal campaign left a permanent scar on the local population.[15] Until the late 1980s, the south Korean state censored public discourse on the 4.3 Uprising. As the state transitioned into procedural democracy after decades of dictatorial rule, consecutive regimes framed the catastrophe as a tragic sacrifice that was necessary to keep evil communist forces at bay. Survivors and witnesses lived side by side with perpetrators on the island, unable to speak about these horrors for fear of reprisal.

In Jeju-do, mudangs understand that their patients seeking peace and healing are not looking only for a cure for a physical illness or personal misfortune. Rather, because nearly every person in Jeju has been directly or indirectly impacted by the 4.3 Uprising, physical, emotional, and psychic pain are perceived as consequences of terror experienced by murdered family members and surviving kin. As "lamentations of the dead," shamanic rites referred to as 씻김굿 (ssitgim-gut) in parts of south Korea and 칠침 (chilch'im) in Jeju-do provide spirits with the opportunity to name and decry their violent deaths.[16] Chilch'im enables spirits to express their unfulfilled desire for safe passage into the afterlife, given that those who have perished by suicide or are killed in war are forced to roam among the living as vengeful spirits. This limbo can be resolved through chilch'im, which clears all barriers to the underworld. By extension, the descendants of these ancestors are protected from the ill will of wandering spirits. Ultimately, the efficacy of these shamanic rituals is dependent on the living's ability to call forth and hold space for all ancestors so that no one in a lineage is neglected.

I am struck by the suggestion that the unresolved sorrows of the deceased can impact the living in malicious ways, enough to destroy the lives of family and friends. So often, ancestors are spoken of in benevolent terms, as if they are angelic guardians looking after the well-being of family and their loved ones. When I learn of this, I worry that my father's spirit has been left unmoored in the realm of the living, unable to transition to the underworld to join his ancestors. I also worry that the resentments my father experienced before his passing remain lodged in this world, leaving a sticky residue that not only haunts but harms. I am reminded of my mother, who tells me weekly about the dreams she has of my father. He stands at a distance from her, with shadows hiding his face as he holds morsels of food that have turned green from rot and mold.

Even as these dreams about my father's vagrant ghost frighten me, I am also moved by the ways in which lamentations of the dead underscore the necessity to mend an entire ancestral community rather than a sole person. This principle speaks to the ways in which a person is never disconnected from the social contexts that shaped them. My understanding of my father is colored by his ancestral relations, and the violence that preceding familial generations survived, including the brutality of Japanese colonialism and US military occupation. While I will never know with absolute certainty, I suspect that such ruptures produced waves of terror that were never judiciously addressed or compassionately held. With my father, these unaddressed histories manifested in several ways, from estranged relations with his family to the ways he attempted to extinguish his own demons through silence and drinking.

I close my eyes and envision what these communal rituals of ancestral grieving could look, feel, and sound like. My mind veers to a performance I witnessed more than two decades ago in Oakland, California, with Dohee Lee, a multimedia artist whose work I discuss in my first book, *Reencounters*. In this performance, Dohee facilitates an improvised kkut, or mourning rite, for ancestors separated from their homes and killed during the Korean War. On the stage, black-and-white archival footage from the war is projected on a large screen. These images are familiar because I have seen different versions before. In one clip, there are exhausted women, children, and elders marching from their villages with large, lumpy sacks wrapped around their thin backs and waists. In another segment, a small child cries next to his father's still body as others pass in their frantic searches for their own children, parents, and siblings. Aerial bombs mutilate the land, leaving burned patches of earth, amputated trees, and misshapen craters. Suddenly, the film stops, and the screen turns black for a split second. The audience holds their breath. When the footage returns to the screen, the film continues at normal speed but in reverse motion. Everything and everyone are moving backward. As Dohee sings a lamentation for the dead, civilians walk in reverse motion toward their villages. The gaping craters are refilled with dirt and grass. In these scenes of alterity, Dohee imagines a life full of abundance where Koreans determine their own destinies. Children are unafraid to run across open fields because there are no subterranean mines, and there is no monstrous scar that severs the Korean Peninsula in half. Families remain together. As this amended footage unravels on the screen, I hear people shifting in their seats and sniffling in their attempts to hold back tears. My lips quiver, and my eyes swell with water when I hear older members in the audience cry out loud.

Rather than yearning for an idealized past or a time before, Dohee's performance conjures a time-space liberated from the debilitating constraints of war and occupation. Even if transient, these visions give credence to a freedom that has been denied to Koreans for so long. They visualize what life could be like without militarized intervention, and

the joy that the living must embrace and work toward. These are not images of the past but of a still-possible present and future. In my conversations with the dead, I whisper to them that I hope this kkut provided sweet balm as they continue to wait for a peace that has eluded them for decades and decades.

....

When I recall this moment, I am grateful to Dohee for mediating a space for me to experience this tender grief as part of an audience. Remembering and feeling a shared anguish that evening put into motion a prayer of reversal for my father, or an elegy of return that consoles:

> *He moves away from the car.*
>
> *He swims across an ocean to the place where he fell in love, where he first learned how to read, where he waited for his father to return home in the evening.*
>
> *He walks alone in a shaded forest of sweet pine trees that promise to protect him.*
>
> *He sleeps in a swaddled cave until it is time.*
>
> *He expands like breath.*
>
> *He returns.*

....

Dohee's performance years ago reminds me of the public dimension of grieving and how this challenges the assumption that mourning is a private act that should only happen behind closed doors. The collaborative grieving that emerged during the kkut reflects how the private and the public are not oppositional. Rather, they share a symbiotic relationship, crisscrossing into and informing one another. In most instances, violence and loss occur against or within the most intimate of spaces, from one's body to the home and community. But individuated acts of racial, gender, and sexual violence are never wholly private because they are caused by and emerge within a social ecology of brutality and inequity.[17] Shared processes of grieving provide a common vocabulary that refutes how certain lives are dismissed as outliers that do not matter in the grand scheme of things. In this challenging work of shared grieving, acknowledging the linkages between the private and the public is crucial to upending the public shaming and guilt that so often discourage survivors of violence from disclosing their experiences in safe and restorative ways—if this is what they wish to do.

Just as important, Dohee shows how the shared work of grieving and naming grievances can offer possibilities beyond the limits of injury. Surviving the catastrophic consequences of war, colonialism, and poverty facilitates empathic resistance and rejoinders to the status quo. Yến Lê Espiritu and Lan Duong, scholars of critical refugee studies, coarticulate this sentiment through a framework they describe as feminist refugee epistemology.[18] Centering the personhoods of those who have been separated and abandoned, a feminist refugee epistemology challenges how Western discourse and media represent survivors of war, including refugees, only as nameless victims in desperate need of charity and tutelage. While underlining the politics of disposability that refugees must navigate for their own survival, Espiritu and Duong celebrate the desires and agency of refugees in their everyday lives. They explore this through the imaginative work of feminist cultural workers and artists who reconfigure private acts, like the act of letter writing in Trinh Mai Thach's installation *Still Quiet*, as politicized forms that refract the "complexities of history and memory, displacement and emplacement."[19] In *Still Quiet,* Thach works with preserved letters penned by Vietnamese refugees who continue to look for missing family, lovers, and children from the war in Vietnam. Despite decades of separation and the US government's refusal to disclose information, Vietnamese survivors continue to search for clues that could reveal the fate of their loved ones. Placed on a small desk equipped with a typewriter, a copy of these letters (typed by Thach) is paired with vertical strips of white chiffon, speckled with black markings, that float from the ceiling. Reminiscent of traditional garments donned by mourners during Vietnamese funerary ceremonies, these long sashes form a gauzy composite of a child's portrait. As audience members move through this suspended curtain of fluttering cloth, they are invited to reflect on their own grief in the silent presence of others. Aesthetic recalibrations like *Still Quiet* envisage ways of public mourning that demonstrate refugees' adamant desire for the disappeared, even as they invite participants to acknowledge the pain and agony of not knowing.

The concept of feminist refugee epistemology is meaningful to me because it reckons with the devastating toll of war and militarized violence, without obscuring the nuances that exceed victimhood. Through writing, I have realized that an integral part of grief-work, or mending my ancestral community, is to uplift the micro- or smaller acts of resistance that were integral to the survival of my diasporic families. The challenge is to do so without masking the naturalized ecosystems of violence that they were entangled in. It can be a delicate balance. When I reflect on my parents' lives in the United States, I am reminded of how hard they worked to survive within a profit-driven society that hungrily extracted, like a thirsty vampire, the blood of their labor, confidence, youthfulness, and vivaciousness. I am reminded, as well, that our lives together, however disjointed and painful, were more than a curated selection of tragic moments. There were joyful evening trips to Disneyland, where my parents, sisters, and I laughed in breathless anticipation as we impatiently awaited our turn to enter the Haunted Mansion. There were lazy Sunday strolls in green parks after the church service in Irvine, and delicious French fries and ice cream from In-N-Out. There were moments of gratitude and elation, like the time my parents cobbled together enough money to purchase a used car for me following my return to California from the East Coast. I honor these moments as much as I remember the evenings of violent rupture between my parents, the eviction from our first home in California, and the financial calamities that crushed my family.

In a surprising way, grieving for my parents has provided a glimpse into their earlier lives in Korea. I picture what they must have been like as children coming of age during a time of war. Everything had to be improvised, reinvented, or rebuilt from scratch. On my mother's side, my grandparents did what they could to support their children during a time of extreme poverty, even if it meant taking on odd jobs with the US military. When I was a child, my mother had a wonderful sense of humor that was at its most vibrant when she shared stories about her love for Hershey's chocolate bars as a little girl. In these tales, she would mention the extra jobs her father took on as a doctor, and the American chocolate bars he received as part of his payment. After he returned home late at night, he would tiptoe into his children's bedrooms to see if they were still studying. In the room that she shared with her two of her sisters, my mother would be hunched over the desk studying for exams while my aunties Youngsuk and Kyung slept in a shared bed. My grandfather would crack the bedroom door open, quietly slipping a chocolate bar into my mother's hands; she became so excited that she had to cover her mouth to muffle her gleeful yelp. Describing herself as her father's favorite child, Mom said that Grandpa would do this often and whisper to her that the sweet treat should be kept a secret so the other children wouldn't become upset. But as soon as my mother opened the wrapping of the chocolate bar and took a bite of its creamy sweetness, the rustling of paper would disturb and wake my aunties. *What are you eating, Young? Give us some!* they squawked.

Mom delighted in telling these stories, transforming her voice to mimic her sisters' deeper voices and laughing along with my sisters and me. I loved hearing these memories because they gestured to moments of joy and pleasure during my mother's childhood. Only in college did I realize that very likely, my grandfather had treated US soldiers, as Hershey's chocolate bars and other coveted sweets could only be accessed at that time at US commissaries or in the black market.

These tales of forbidden sweetness point to my maternal grandparents' creativity and their determination to maintain a sense of security for their children. They also hint to me that my mother's sense of humor possibly developed as a muscular form of resistance that buffered her from the uncertainties of everyday life in a war-ravaged Korea.

. . . .

Several months after my dad passed away, I emailed Jane Jin Kaisen to seek guidance about grieving and mourning rituals. Like Dohee, Jane is a visual artist whose versatile work has been shared in my scholarship and writing over the years. She is also a trusted comrade who has offered sage advice on projects, and someone I have collaborated with on public talks and editorial work. I sought Jane's guidance because her artistic oeuvre focuses on memory, migration, borders, and protest in Jeju and the Korean diaspora—and more specifically, the 4.3 Uprising, the Korean War, and Korean transnational adoption. More recently, Jane's film and photography projects engage Korean shamanic rituals and spiritual mediations in Jeju-do, where her birth family is from.

In her gentle response to me, Jane shares the voice of Koh Sunahn, a revered shaman in Jeju-do whom she worked closely with until Koh's death in 2019. Koh was a survivor of the 4.3 Uprising and a student of Jane's grandfather in Jeju. In one of the tracks that Jane shares with me, Koh's chanting uplifts the spirits of the dead, including those killed during the 4.3 Uprising. When I listen to Koh's voice in these recordings, I am moved by her fluctuating voice, punctuated by silence and staccato breaths. Sound and listening are vital to Jane's films, which are often filled with shamanic singing, bell chimes, the ethereal *whoosh* of ocean waves, and overlapping languages. Somehow, Koh's somber lamentations evoke for me the simultaneity of pain and cathartic relief that characterizes the visceral experience of mourning.

Segments of these chants, as well as Koh Sunahn's life, are featured in Jane's single-channel film, *Community of Parting* (2019). This experimental film is structured around the Korean myth of the Princess Bari, or Bari Gongju, popularly understood as the origin story of Korean shamanism. Bari is the seventh daughter of King Ogu and Queen Gildae, who are despondent that Bari is born as a girl. In response, they place her delicate body into a stone box, offering Bari to the freezing waters of the Hwangcheon River. But unbeknownst to her parents, Bari survives this act of abandonment. Years later, when the king and queen are deathly ill, Bari volunteers to travel to the underworld to retrieve life-saving water that eventually cures her parents of their illness. While traditional renderings of this myth celebrate Bari's filial loyalty, Jane reconfigures the myth into a story of disavowal: Rather than receiving her father's gift of half of his kingdom, Bari chooses to remain at the threshold between the living and the dead to guide souls in their afterlives. She becomes the knowledge bearer of the dead, and the mediator between the earthly and spiritual realms. To this day, Bari Gongju remains the archetype of shamans in Korea.

Like feminist refugee epistemology, *Community of Parting* honors the situated agency in an ancestor's life without romanticizing and diminishing the hardships they survived or didn't survive. The film focuses on the myth of Bari Gongju to constellate different histories of abandonment and transformation. These diasporic histories include that of Korean transnational adoption, a diasporic community that Jane is a part of; the 4.3 Uprising, including Koh Sunahn's story of death and survival; the Koryo-saram, or the descendants of Koreans forcibly relocated from the Russian Far East to Central Asia under Joseph Stalin's regime; zainichi, or ethnic Koreans born and raised in Japan; and Koreans in the United States and western Europe. The juxtaposition of these narratives includes the nonhuman as well, ranging from the undetonated mines that sleep along the terrestrial edge of the Korean demilitarized zone, to deserted medical facilities that housed sex workers accused of infecting US servicemen with venereal disease, to unsettled spirits who cry in the forests, mountains, and rivers.

The significance of these stories is not so much the residual sorrow that remains after violence. Rather, *Community of Parting* emphasizes how abandonment can foster sensibilities that may not be otherwise possible. When people survive abandonment and other devastating losses, they can be transformed by these experiences because they potentiate an empathic capacity to feel and accept what others refuse to, or cannot, grasp. This emotional threshold between life and death is what distinguishes the abandoned from others: While this metamorphosis produces an outcast status, it also generates a fragile sense of affinity, even solidarity, among survivors and the abandoned. Near the end of the film, scholar Anja Sunhyun Michaelsen suggests the following: "I understood social death to be the ultimate abandonment, but then the shamanist approach would be that that opens and enables. If you are outside of conventional notions of history and conventional notions of space and time, you can see different things. You need this kind of death to be able to have a more complex image of the world and of its relations. So, abandonment there becomes a completely different concept."

Koh Sunahn's life and work are testaments to this. While she navigated a difficult life as a shaman in Jeju-do, Koh's gifts enabled her to be a keeper of memories that very few are trusted with. Koh was sought by those who yearned for their children, parents, lovers, and ancestors to find rest and closure, so that they themselves could find peace. This is evident in *Community of Parting* when Koh facilitates an encounter between Jane and her deceased grandparents. Jane's face is turned away from the camera, but her back quivers as Koh requests the presence of her grandparents in the room. What is remarkable about this shamanic ritual is the way that Koh conjures a genealogy of state violence that sutures Jane to her grandparents. The connection that Koh offers through this spiritual interface is not that of biological ties but the social death that Jane's grandparents and Jane both experienced in distinct yet related ways. Her grandparents were survivors of the 4.3 Uprising, while Jane is a transnational adoptee, an enterprise that originated, with significant help from Western humanitarian aid workers and missionaries, during the period of US military governance in Korea (1945–48). As a baby, Jane was removed from her family of origin and sent to live thousands of miles away in a radically different cultural, social, linguistic, and racial context.

Koh's ritual suggests that these incommensurable experiences are connected through overlapping conditions that led to the Cold War emergence of a south Korean state. Both experiences are consequences of a political calculus through which the south Korean government, with undeterred support from the United States, determined which bodies needed to be sacrificed for the sake of anticommunist capitalist development. Through this mediated encounter between Jane and her grandparents, Koh suggests that ancestors can alleviate the heartache of their descendants by relinquishing their own sorrow and anger. "Dear Grandfather and Grandmother," she says. "If you have pent-up hearts... please release it and then this descendant's pent-up heart will be released too."

Although I have viewed *Community of Parting* many times, watching it after my father's death elicited a response I had not experienced before. Much of my grieving, up to that point, had been about the combustive circumstances surrounding my father's death and my mother's hospitalization. But *Community of Parting* compelled me to consider the transformation that occurs through and alongside banishment and severance. In the most unexpected sense, these experiences can germinate improvised forms of defiance, no matter how seemingly minor or subtle. Acknowledging these smaller forms of daily resistance—while a far cry from acts of so-called empowerment—allows me to remember both of my parents, especially my father, in more complicated ways.

Though he never expressed this to me in so many words, my father held ambivalent if not antagonistic feelings toward the United States. During his forty-plus years in the country, he resisted learning English, disliked "American" foods unless they were served alongside Korean dishes, and was distrustful of institutions like the US legal system. Al-

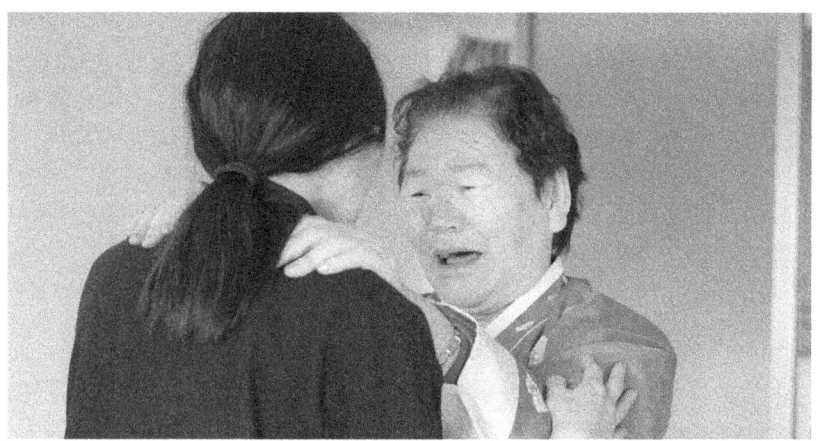

though limited time and access to resources influenced these preferences, I now wonder whether his choices at least in part reflected a stubborn refusal to assimilate or perform an Asian American model-minority identity. This speculation departs from much of the existing Asian American literature on grief as theorized through concepts like racial melancholia. In this body of scholarship, melancholia is described as a by-product of the white capitalist origins of the United States. While the United States has long demanded that its residents assimilate into a white heterosexual society, this task is impossible for Asian Americans because their bodies are perpetually legislated as outside of the national citizenry. For Asian Americans, their yearning for acceptance and the ultimate futility of this desire translate into an abjection that is absorbed by the unconscious. This psychic loss is then transmitted to younger generations, who are haunted by an intergenerational grief whose origins they cannot name or decipher.[20]

But for my father, the grief he experienced during his lifetime was not because he desired to call the United States his home. He was, in fact, resistant to this demand. For different reasons, he never mentioned south Korea as a place of refuge he longed for or desired to return to. Dad, then, seemed caught in a liminal space between two less-than-ideal options, neither of which he was loyal to. This disavowal made him an aberration among other Korean fathers I grew up with in Orange County. These fathers, at least in public, were ambitious doctors, lawyers, real estate agents, or corporate presidents who leisurely played golf at country clubs every Friday and Saturday and took their families on nice vacations to Europe or Korea every summer. Dressed in their expensive pressed suits, these fathers, after Sunday service, wouldn't be shy about sharing their yearly bonuses from their businesses and their ability to send their children to the most exclusive private schools in Los Angeles. When I searched for my parents after the service, my dad would often be standing in a circle with these fathers. With his hands stuffed into the pockets of his suit jacket, he would faintly smile, nod, and make small talk, but mostly, he would be looking down or into the distance as if he wanted to be elsewhere.

In some ways, my father resembled what Lisa Marie Cacho describes as a "deviant subject" in the context of American neoliberalism, which centers hyperproductivity, white middle-class status, financial success, and focused ambition as core values.[21] Dad didn't have lofty aspirations, he was terrible with money, he lived more for the present than for the future, and he mostly worked blue-collar jobs that barely paid (or didn't pay) the bills. For other Koreans in my life, including childhood friends and their parents, my father exemplified someone who had not made it in the United States. Dad's death made evident the aspirational hierarchy of value that constitutes social worth in a punishing racist capitalist society. He was appraised as an object of nonvalue, which uplifted a criterion that deemed only some as valuable and worthy of love and care. In other words, my dad, in his life and death, is a "bad example to follow, [but] a good lesson to learn."[22] Sometimes, I wonder whether this perception is one silently shared by my mother's friends and family, though they would never say such a thing because of their love for my sisters and me. I am afraid that they might consider my father an unworthy person, so much so that when I am with my mother's family during gatherings, I hold myself from crying, screaming, and expressing the depth of my grief. What does it mean to mourn for someone perceived as ungrievable because he failed to meet every expectation as a good sibling (or sibling-in-law), spouse, worker, and citizen?

Returning to *Community of Parting* and Korean cosmologies of death and mourning has placed this question at the heart of my grieving process. Sitting with this query through writing and ritual has made perceptible the stratified complexities of family relationships, personhood, and grief. To love and mourn for my father is to reckon with the devastating mistakes he made, while also acknowledging the conditions that influenced his life. Somehow, holding these two truths at the same time—and giving myself the latitude to be angry at his actions, while also naming the barriers that hampered Dad's life—clarifies for me the ways my father mattered to me beyond a commodified understanding of value and worth.

When I hold space to acknowledge my love for my father despite his faults and blunders, I often think about the spontaneous eulogy my twin sister, Cris, gave during his memorial service. While Coleen and I had carefully prepared eulogies for that day, it was the poet among us who shared the most powerful remembrance of our father. Cris had not been planning to share anything, but after Coleen and I spoke, she was moved to recall a memory from our childhood. She and I were eight or nine, and we had just joined our elementary school's band; Cris opted for the clarinet while I gravitated toward the flute. Our family couldn't afford the nice and shiny instruments that all of the other children in our class seemed to have, so for some time, we borrowed from the school's music teacher until Cris and I were asked to purchase our own flute and clarinet. Cris, in particular, pined for a beautiful wooden clarinet because it was able to produce deeply sonorous sounds. It was also much more expensive than its plastic counterpart. When Cris asked my mother about this, Mom looked embarrassed as she told Cris that we could only afford a plastic clarinet.

On the Saturday that our parents took us to the music instrument store, Cris lingered in the parking lot as she tugged at and tightly held on to my father's hand. Sensing her disappointment, Dad knelt down and hugged her. *Let's go in and see what we can do, okay? Maybe we can bargain for the wooden clarinet,* he gently said. Thirty minutes later, Cris and I skipped out of the store with our new instruments in tow: a nickel silver flute for me and a wooden clarinet for my sister. Somehow, my father had managed to "bargain" with the store's manager for a lower price. While I'm uncertain how he did this, I imagine that he bartered with the manager and offered a discount on expensive furniture at his shop, or maybe he promised to pay him later in installments. Whatever he did, Cris left the music store that day with a toothy grin on her face.

My sister's story is a meaningful reminder of how my father navigated the anxiety-ridden conditions of capitalism by hustling his way through and against a system that always seemed stacked against us. Dad refused to follow the rules and found his own way out, even if it meant scheming against, ignoring, or breaking with established protocol. While these tactics often backfired with disastrous results for our family—and though these decisions were not always altruistic or selfless on his part—I like to think of Dad as someone who did not want to give in to the racist limitations, the painful rejections, and the humiliations of *no* that so many migrant and refugee families confront on a daily basis in this country.

Grieving for my parents as part of the Korean diaspora also elucidates how I experience time and temporality in relation to my family. In writing about my parents' histories, I realize that the militarized colonial ruptures experienced by Korea and Koreans have not produced only a sense of chronic deferral. Additionally, I experience time as a parallax, a different kind of return, as if it is simultaneously moving forward and standing still at any given moment. For my parents, their migration to the United States was informed by a desire to start a fresh new life away from a place they associated with war, political instability, familial tensions, and visceral reminders of poverty. At the same, these experiences constituted who they became and how they loved, formed their family, and eked out a living in the United States. The temporal and spatial distance my parents craved, or the desire to move forward and far away, was impossible because the animated dimensions of war, familial strife, resentment, and psychic pain were seared into their bodies.

This contradictory juxtaposition between the urgent desire to leave something behind and the unattainability of this dream infiltrates how I think, feel, and write about Korea and my family. For a long time, I considered myself close to my parents. As it turns out, they are two people whom I deeply loved (still love) and hardly knew at all. I write about the ways in which grief and grievance are experienced in the Korean diaspora through my ancestral lineages. Yet the myriad stories I've shared have congealed through the prism of speculation, insinuation, and translation. The histories, sounds, feelings, and images communicated in these pages are soberingly real and impactful, as much as they are imaginatively summoned through lingering questions that will never be contended with in a definitive way.

For the first anniversary of my father's passing, I prepared jesa for him to honor him as an ancestor. As someone who was not taught nor raised with these ancestral rituals and had never performed them before, I was nervous that I would falter in ways I could not even articulate at the time.[23] Traditionally, jesa ceremonies are intricate, with a detailed sequence of steps and protocols that only specific people in each family can perform. I wanted to respect these protocols while also recognizing that there were gendered elements I rejected, and other aspects I could not practice on my own. But after speaking with friends, I learned of how they respectfully drew on these ancestral rituals in ways that resonated with their own locations and access to different religious practices, knowledges, and political commitments.

One friend, CK, shared with me how learning about these mourning rituals from her mother and relatives provided a reliable structure and space for her grief following her father's passing. Given her parents' commitment to Catholicism, these jesa rituals were interwoven into Christian funerary ceremonies. "After [my dad's passing] and before his burial, church members came in and out of my mother's home lighting incense and chanted prayers 위령기도 (연도). I'm not religious myself, but the traditional Korean chanting cadence was soothing during those days when things felt overwhelming."[24]

Another friend, Eunice, described for me her mourning rituals to mark the death of her mother during the global COVID-19 pandemic. Eunice and her 이모 (eemos), or maternal aunties, complemented the jesa ceremony with Buddhist practices of chanting and meditation for forty-nine days immediately following her mother's death. In Theravada and Mahayana lineages of Buddhism, this stretch of time is significant because it is the transient period in which a person's spirit is held between death and rebirth. Referred to as 천도재, or ch'ŏndojae, in Korean, this period determines the next life cycle for a spirit as they are reincarnated into a different form or attain enlightenment. In a short essay she graciously wrote for me when I asked her how she grieved for her mother, Eunice describes her process in this way:

> I am deeply grateful for the Korean and Buddhist traditions around mourning, as they gave me some structure and container for us to move through this all. These inherited traditions have deep wisdom. Making an altar and chanting the namu amita bul sutra for the 49 days after [my mother's] death was a welcome anchor. My eemos in Korea told me that they were doing the same, so it felt nice to know that my mom would hear these loving messages from many directions. The moment after I created the altar in our living room—covered with a blanket that one of our friends had woven, decorated with flowers

that more friends had sent—and set my mother's photo at the top, it felt like I had, in a small way, created a portal to my mom.²⁵

In their descriptions of mourning practices, a third comrade, "ENP," noted the ways they conjoined jesa with other cultural lineages to grieve for and honor Palestinian lives lost during a time of genocide, cruelty, and annihilating violence. Creating an altar by and for queer and transgender BIPOC members in Los Angeles, ENP and others combined jesa with 고사 (gosa), or offerings to the land, water, and air. Participants gathered to offer words, song, food, photographs, and handwritten notes to the altar space in support of Palestinian life and liberation. Others integrated mourning practices from their own cultural traditions that spanned from sitting with the altar to offering flowers and medicinal plants to using prayer beads in their lamentations. I found this touching as these grieving practices foreground the historical connections of struggle between Koreans and Palestinians, given that both peoples have sought—through radically distinct and shared conditions, such as the division of land and family separation—decolonization, sovereignty, and freedom from militarized rule and occupation during this past century.²⁶ As ENP observes, "It was moving to be able to offer from spirit in this open way: to the martyrs of Palestine and all witnesses to injustice, to the land of Palestine suffering the impacts of violent systems, and to each other and the land we ourselves are on."²⁷

These examples of jesa in conjunction with ancestral practices of grieving in and beyond the Korean diaspora demonstrate the ways in which rituals provide an entry point, rather than a fixed script, to name and care for our dead. Similarly to the diasporic rituals mediated by Dohee Lee and Jane Jin Kaisen, CK's, Eunice's, and ENP's reformulated practices queer the most traditional elements of jesa. Historically, jesa has been facilitated by the eldest son or cisgender man in the family, while women were permitted to participate only through the preparation of ceremonial food. For some today, jesa continues to reaffirm filial duty and hierarchies by supporting family succession through a patrilineal lineage.²⁸ But these elements of jesa are not unconditional, nor does jesa demand absolute obedience to parental authority. Rather, the most pivotal aspect of jesa is to "revere the source of life" and to honor the living's relations with their dead, however one might know, love, and understand their ancestral lines.²⁹

As I organized my father's first jesa, I held this principle of revering the source of life at the very center of the ceremonial plan. For Dad, the source of life was not only a circle of people whom he loved but also a beloved community of animals, trees, and plants who accepted him as he was. When he was still able to see and walk, he would stroll daily to a nearby park with my parents' dog, Shelly, and speak with and hug a majestic oak tree he befriended during his many visits. He did this so often that once, a woman observing my father from a nearby playground called the Montclair police, believing that he was mentally ill. In honor of his devotion to plants and foliage, I placed onto my home altar two shorn branches from a white sage plant that my partner Dan has lovingly grown and nurtured in our front yard. We placed these fragrant branches in a light green celadon vase that Cris had brought back for me from her trip to northern Korea over a decade ago, to signify the land that my father's family is from.

Alongside dishes that included savory strips of smoked dried squid and a hearty bowl of tofu and pumpkin stew, my father's photograph was placed next to my paternal grandparents' portrait to symbolize their shared ancestral lineage. The incense smoke and soju invite ancestral spirits from above and below to meet and gather at the altar, while the dishes of food are provided as offerings to feed and nourish the dead. On the other side of my father's photograph, I placed an agate stone gifted to me by the poet Don Mee Choi. I first met Don Mee during her trip to Los Angeles in April 2018, which overlapped with a historic summit held between north and south Korean leaders just south of the military demarcation line. During her talk at the University of California, Los Angeles, which I co-organized, Don Mee read to the audience several poems from her working manuscript, DMZ Colony, which was eventually published in 2020.[30]

Following this visit, Don Mee mailed me a package that included a beautiful green stone with smooth and jagged edges that caught shimmers of light in its crevices. A translucent sea green color with slants of the lightest brown distributed throughout its surface and body, this stone hails from Marfa, a desert city in Texas that is rich in mineral reserves because it was submerged under the ocean centuries ago. Somehow, this knowledge that this small stone had been molded by an aqueous past and had, over a millennium, survived and morphed to become a crystalline part of the fiery desert landscape resonated with me. I hoped that the presence of this subterranean mineral stone would console my father's spirit by showing him how impermanence and departure are not only unavoidable but also necessary to transition to the next part of our journey.

While I meticulously planned for my father's jesa weeks before the ceremony, even going as far as creating a detailed program for the ritual, the day of the ceremony was disrupted by a chain of disturbances. A friend's dog we were caring for that week suddenly became ill overnight, keeping Dan and me awake until the wee hours of the morning. Tired and groggy, Dan and I fought that morning over something so minuscule that the source of the conflict now escapes my memory. While I had known that my mother and sisters could not join me for the ceremony, the sobering realization that I would be the only one from my family to facilitate this ritual on the first anniversary of my father's passing created a weighted sense of responsibility. Whether a fair assessment or not, I felt that it was up to me to ensure that my father's spirit would find peace and ease as he continued to cross the bridge into the underworld.

But as Dan and I performed the jesa while our dogs, Danbi and Shelly, quietly observed from a distance, I realized that these interruptions were my father's way of communicating with us. It reminded me of a similar disruption that occurred on the day of my father's memorial service in January 2023. While Dan and I were preparing to attend the service at my Uncle Sukjin's house, Danbi mischievously swallowed a sock. Dan was forced to make an emergency visit to our veterinarian's office during the middle of a heavy rainstorm, or "bomb cyclone," as some call it, and missed the service altogether.

My father might have been invisible during his jesa, but his spirit was in the room. Just like the bittersweet story that Heonik Kwon shares in *After the Korean War* of the two spoons inching toward one another during jesa, the morning's interruptions were an emergent form of testimony reconfigured into a string of mishaps that the living could see, listen to, and witness. Maybe my father was trying to express to us his sorrow and anger, or perhaps he was communicating his desire for me to let him go. After the ceremony, I sat alone in front of the altar for some time, watching the curling trails of incense smoke perfume and dissipate into the air. I silently shared with my father-ancestor that I hoped he was feeling less burdened in his afterlife and that he would eventually return to a place where he could finally sleep.

Let us live like
an endangered species
carefully and intentionally

POSTHUMOUS TRANSLATION

Translation is a map, a mode that can trigger endless crossings from one party to another, "neither of whom has seen."
—DON MEE CHOI, *Translation Is a Mode=Translation Is an Anti-Neocolonial Mode*

FOR FORTY-NINE DAYS between June and July 2023, I wrote to my father every day. The forty-nine-day period following a loved one's death is significant in Buddhism because a person's spirit is held within a border-space as they wait to enter a cycle of rebirth. Letter writing is something my friend Eunice offered to her own mother following her death. While I was unable to write to my father immediately after he died, Eunice encouraged me to put onto paper the reservoir of words I held for him. In hindsight, I realize how crucial this correspondence was for my mourning process: In his absence, it permitted me to put into language the things I wanted to express to him.

In these letters to my dad, I offered memories I had of him and our time together, as well as questions, assumptions, and regrets I've held on to. In several of these letters, I inquired about his parents and siblings, hoping that his relationships with them as ancestral kin, rather than as son and brother, would be compassionate and forgiving. On other days, I described to him, in the most mundane terms possible, the flow of my day and the things I've come to love or detest. And on still other days, these letters were sparse, including only a phrase that described the day's weather or a dream I had the night before. The sporadic white spaces diffused throughout these pages are as much a part of my correspondence as the words shared with my father. Even in his death, there are things I find difficult to say out loud to him. These islands of blank space are a testament to this sentiment.

For several months, I dropped these notes into a large circular glass vase that sat on my home altar next to my father's portrait. One by one, these unopened letters accumulated. On December 5, 2023, following my father's first jesa, I burned these letters in my backyard. As I watched pieces of paper catch flame and melt into flakes of ash, I thought about the parallels between this transformation and the unfolding of my grief. Grieving is overwhelming, even annihilating. It also mediates a distillation process that cleans, clears, and releases. Grieving clarified for me that the eruptive breaks in my family are demonstrative of historical fault lines that stretch for miles underneath the molten surface of timespace. This transfiguration from paper to glowing ember signals something else: the rendering of written words into communicative elements that can be deciphered by my father as an ancestor. The dead listen and speak in languages that differ from those spoken, heard, and understood by the living. I imagine that the burning of these letters translated my words into murmuring frequencies, like the submerged churning of ocean waves, that our ancestors are able to receive. Fire can annihilate, even as it cleans, clears, and releases.

Maybe because of my impulse to preserve everything or a fear that these words would disappear from my memory, I photographed each letter to my father after writing them. When I revisited these notes through images saved on my phone, I was struck by the ways through which I experienced them. For whatever reason, only a fraction of the words on each page jumped out at me, catching my attention. As I read through each image, I wrote down the collection of words that remained with me, almost as if they were emotional residues. This selection of words felt intimate and intuitive to me, as if a visceral sensibility was organically crystallizing as a method to engage disappeared words and objects that no longer exist in their original form.

When I share this improvised process with Cris, she tells me that it is reminiscent of a poetic practice referred to as erasure poetry. In this lyrical form, specific words are removed, redacted, or erased from existing prose to generate a new constellation of words, or even a wholly different poem. The revised spacing and redactions themselves are an integral part of the amended poem. I am moved by Cris's description of erasure poetry because it resonates with the ways I have navigated grief after my parents' transformations. Disappearance and departure are not complete erasures. They instead create different forms of presence, expression, and relationality that may seem, at least initially, beyond perceptibility. In the most surprising way, writing akin to erasure poetry surfaced as a praxis of posthumous translation through this ritual, or an intimate way to feel for words that have crossed from the living to the dead. Perhaps these othered notes are my father's way, as an ancestor, of responding to me through words I can only now listen to and hold.

As a form of return, the following is a selection of ten notes written to my father in 2023, rerendered through the act of posthumous translation in 2024.

JUNE 29, 2023

What did you fear the most, Dad?

                                    Why did you drive the car that day?

....

JUNE 26, 2023

                        I thought about

    the intentions you   held,

even if you could not follow through

                      you loved   so much.

Love,

                                                Crystal

....

JULY 4, 2023

                    did you like fireworks? I can't

remember

            I hate the 4th of July

Is there
            a sliver of

memory

                  to remember.

....

JUNE 28, 2023

I'm unsettled tonight.

                      I'm like Mom that way—

       I become
Hypervigilant

....

JUNE 27, 2023

how   terrifying and exhausting

          for you

and Mom   this fucked-up country

                    the violence of capitalism.

this system doesn't reward people like us.

(unfinished)—

....

JULY 28, 2023

          I was trying

to let go of hard memories

It is impossible.

....

JUNE 22, 2023

Forgive me.

I forgive you.

....

JULY 15, 2023

I   hold you in my heart.

With all your complexities,

> Your daughter,
> Crystal

....

JULY 9, 2023

Dear Dad—

I saw Mom this morning

I want to
                             directly

experience her as she is now

....

JUNE 23, 2023

    these moments seem to be disappearing faster than I imagined.

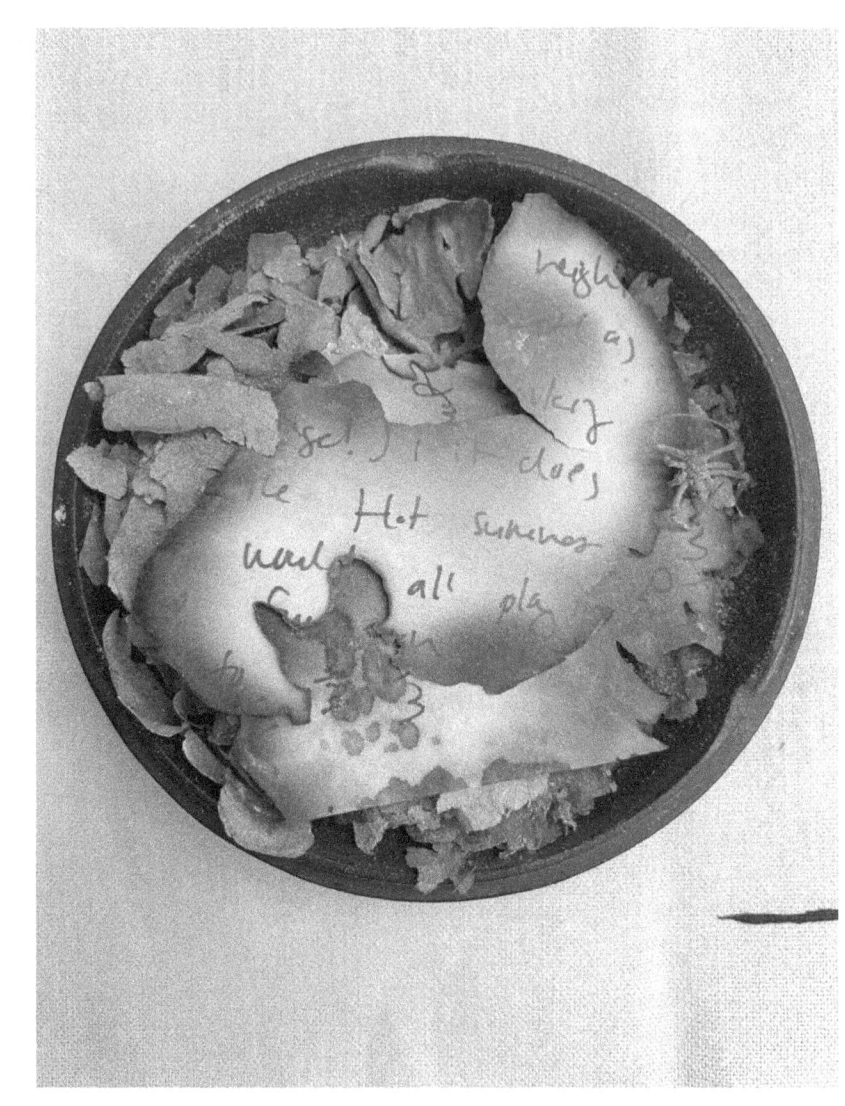

INVOCATION

A PROTECTION SPELL

Cristiana Kyung-hye Baik

Let us speak
in our diasporic language—
whispers from a wind phone
harnessed
by the pull of the moon.

Let us dispossess
    the gods we pray to
    so that we can have our sanity,
    our bodies, our minds,
the present on our terms.

Let us find moments
    to sit together by a quiet stream,
up the riverbank through
bulrush and thorn, waiting
for the high water, without fear,
together.

Let us have too much whiskey,
and fall asleep to dream
of beaches,
bridges, a long escape
of land that knows
no borders except
with water.

Let us remember
the burning of homes,
bombs, the eternal separations,

which a generation later,
translate to slamming doors,
   broken glass, our ancestors' screams—

ghosts on water.

 Let us remember
Grandmother, who in silence kept
company with her ghost—
   her sister
whom she walked along
the Sŏngch'ŏn River,
함흥평야, daily, who vanished
in the midst of war, like too many
of our ancestors.

Let us belong to our ghosts,
and them to us,
so that we take their blessings,
and we may know of the dangerous
dreams of their youth.

Let us also bless you, ancestors,
as you sleeplessly walk
along what is called the DMZ,
that rotting
border of the US's
cavalier contempt.

Let us know the intimacy
of abandonment, as we look
for your homes,

your mothers, fathers, sisters,
brothers, lost
in this unending war.

Let our ancestors' losses be our ability,
our autobiography,
so that we sing and write
in our diasporic language
of ashes, water, wind, fire.

Let us live like
an endangered species,
carefully and intentionally
forging life like a revealed result—

the light carried by the whispers
from the wind phone.

ACKNOWLEDGMENTS

I write these words during a time of annihilating violence. In the thirteen months since the Trump V.2 administration came to power in the United States, we have witnessed an accelerated dismantling of protections for people and the environment. Immigrant and refugee populations have been placed in especially precarious positions (even more so than before), with heightened rates of detention, disappearance, and deportation tearing communities apart. While government threats against undocumented people are not new, the Trump administration has targeted permanent residents who have criticized the Israeli state's genocidal campaign in Gaza—an endeavor fueled by the generosity of US monetary aid. On March 8, 2025, Mahmoud Khalil, a student at Columbia University who led campus protests against Israel's catastrophic policies, was seized by US Immigration and Customs Enforcement (ICE) agents. After 104 days in detention—and only after mass mobilization and protest—Khalil was released on June 20, 2025, with no pending criminal charges. In the meantime, other students across US university campuses have been kidnapped and detained. Against this backdrop of surveillance and carceral violence is the most sorrowful realization of all: Since October 2023, an estimated seventy thousand Palestinians have been murdered by Israeli military forces, though this number is likely a tiny fraction of the actual number of deaths. Palestinians in the West Bank are under constant military scrutiny and settler surveillance, with skyrocketing rates of home demolition and displacement destroying any semblance of stability in their everyday lives.

It is crucial to acknowledge these conditions because this sobering moment has undeniably imprinted itself on and motivated my writing. How could it not? The utter precarity of this time, punctuated by genocide and state terror, has foregrounded the necessity to create with resounding joy and a resolute commitment to love and resistance. With this in mind, my writing emerges from a place of solidarity, so much so that my emotionally inflected work is inseparable from other practices—

including protest, prayer, ritual, and communal care and nourishment—in the hopes that we remain steadfast in our survival. I am writing to remain present in the *now*, even while the intensity of historical violence and its animated reverberations force me to pause and remember my breath. I am writing against and beyond the institutionalization of knowledge, which too often disciplines us students and scholars into fearing our imagination and freedom.

In this process of breathing, writing, and creating at such a time, I have been cared for and held by many. I want to thank my sisters, Cristiana Kyung-hye Baik and Coleen Eun-hye Baik, for their love and patience as I conjured this book during an impossible period. Despite being pressed for time, Cristiana contributed a powerful protection spell that concludes this book. My appreciation extends to Cristiana's partner, Steven Tran, and their beautiful children, Iseul and Bomi, who have brought tremendous joy, mischief, and laughter into our lives. I want to thank my mother, Young Ok Baik, and my late father, Inki Baik, for surviving the best that they could. My mother's family, including Aunties Kyung, Youngsuk, Jonghyun, and Gongja, and my late Uncle Sukyoon and Uncle Sukjin, made sure my sisters and I were taken care of following my father's death and my mother's hospitalization. Although the words that fill these pages might be painful for my family to read, my hope is that it will move us to acknowledge the destructive and long-term impact that war, division, and capitalism have had on our everyday lives.

My partner, Daniel Kikuo Ichinose, is the most important person in my life; I am grateful for his calm and grounded energy and the full life we have built together with Danbi and Shelly. Dan's family, including Auntie Ruby and Uncle Bob, Auntie Audrey and Uncle Mike, and Auntie Nerissa, have always treated me as if I was one of their own. I am beyond grateful for the meaningful time we have spent together. My gratitude extends to Dan's cousin, Alec MacDonald, who read an early version of a chapter and offered invaluable advice. Travers and Juanita Ichinose, along with beautiful Teo and Asha, are an extended part of our home in Southern California; I love them with all my heart.

My chosen family are an integral part of my life; without them, I am uncertain whether I would have been able to finish this book. Wendy Cheng and Eric Wat were my very first readers; while I was initially hesitant to share this new body of work, their love, encouragement, and thoughtful feedback expanded my understanding of scholarly writing. I had the privilege of workshopping a complete manuscript draft with the most brilliant group of trusted friends and interlocutors: Anjali Nath, Caren Kaplan, Vinh Nguyen, and Jinah Kim. I cannot underscore enough how much their patient reading and generous feedback supported the reworking of the manuscript. My dear friend and colleague Latipa also read a chapter draft and gently encouraged me to break with academic conventions; I am constantly in awe of her courage. I am thankful to Clara Han, who invited me to share this work at Johns Hopkins University in fall 2024; Clara's writing proved to be influential for the crafting of this book. Mike Baccam provided generous feedback during an early phase of this project. I am grateful to Clare Counihan, who is the most thoughtful indexer I could have asked for. Kimberly Miller is an extraordinary copyeditor, and I am grateful for her incisive feedback. While searching for my paternal grandfather's biographical information in Korean, Ju Hui Judy Han and Jeongsu Shin provided crucial resources that allowed me to locate his scholarly work. Jeongsu provided critical translation support as I sought to read portions of an intellectual biography written about my grandfather. I am indebted to both Judy and Jeongsu for their translation support and care.

There is a community of close friends who kept me sane these past several years. This includes members of the TK Drama Club, aka Wendy Cheng, Jinah Kim, and Aimee Bahng. Their love, sense of humor, and friendship have meant the world to me, and I am so glad they are a part of my life. I am grateful to Anjali Nath, whom I communicate with nearly every day; she is my closest writing and thought partner. Caren Kaplan, Andrea Miller, and Javier Arbona have provided steadfast camaraderie, laughter, and smart conversation during a dystopian time. I am especially grateful to Caren for modeling such caring and present mentorship. In California and beyond, I remain inspired by friends who continue to organize, teach, write, resist, refuse, caregive, and create during this difficult time. These friends include Elizabeth Sunwoo, Enji Chung, Mari Ryono, Yoon Ju Ellie Lee, Mimi E. Kim, Gloria Chan Sook Kim, Yumi Pak, Ju Hui Judy Han, Jennifer Jihye Chun, Tina Kim, Sujin Lee, Preeti Sharma, Eric Wat, Eunice Hyunhye Cho, Cat Pyun, Janice Cho, and Kyunjin Lee. Narae Park, Ara Kim, Jio Kim, Gonji Lee, Karam Ahn, and Haejin Bang provided crucial coordination and translation support as my sisters and I sought care for our mother. I am grateful for their care and generosity.

Three decades ago, I met a circle of friends in rural Williamstown with whom I continue to be in touch. Even with the ebbs and flows of our long-distance friendships, I am forever inspired by the courage and creativity of Susie Yeo, Janet Curran, Ja Young Ahn-Williams, Joo Han, Naomi Jackson, and Katherine E. Foo. In the past fifteen years, I am fortunate to have learned from brilliant scholars, artists, writers, survivors, archivists, and organizers who have taught me more than I could ever reciprocate. This includes Sarah Fong, Joo Ok Kim, Davorn Sisavath, Nic Ramos, Simeon Man, Alfred Flores, Kirisitina Sailiata, Youngoh Jung, Lena Sze, Amita Manghnani, Shannon O'Neill, Elizabeth Son, Minju Bae, Juyeon Rhee, Workshops 4 Gaza, the After Violence Project, Creative Interventions, Jane Jin Kaisen, Emily Hue, Chris Fan, Amy Guey-Sun Chen, Dohee Lee, Don Mee Choi, Lily Wong, Meklit Hadero, Christine Bacareza Balance, Laura Hyun Yi Kang, Mark Padoongpatt, Monisha Das Gupta, Stephen Hong Sohn, meital yaniv, Fanny García, Dao Tran, Thuy Vo Dang, mads lê, Hentyle Yapp, Monica Kim, Christine Hong, Kimberly Chang, and Svetlana Kitto.

Thank you to the following artists for permitting me to reproduce their original work (or images that document their work) in this book: Sun Young Kang, for allowing me to use images of her installation *neither here nor there* for the book's cover art; Enji Chung, for allowing me to reproduce five of their original photographs that depict the 2024 solar eclipse; Jane Jin Kaisen, for allowing me to include a still frame from her powerful film *Community of Parting*; and Dohee Lee, for gifting me with the opportunity to include a photograph that documents one of her public performances (captured by Scott Tsuchitani). I am grateful to Kaylie Hopper, Michelle 진아 Song, and Lola Mui, who encouraged me to take better care of my body, mind, and spirit. I am galvanized by the Palestinian American Research Center and all PARC faculty fellows who have provided me with the gift of solidarity during a turbulent time.

While the university is a difficult place to work at, I am proud to be a member of the Department of Gender and Sexuality Studies (GSST) at the University of California, Riverside. I am especially grateful for the care and support provided by my GSST colleagues Brandon Andrew Robinson, Sherine Hafez, Jack Cáraves, Jade Sasser, Katja Guenther, Tamara Ho, and Liz Rubio. Emily Hue, Donatella Galella, Xóchitl Chávez, Gloria Chan Sook Kim, Megan Asaka, Latipa, Brandon Andrew Robinson, Jack Cáraves, Sherine Hafez, Anthea Kraut, Imani Kai Johnson, Liz Przybylski, Keith Miyake, Emma Stapley, Liz Rubio, taisha paggett,

María Regina Firmino-Castillo, Sarita See, Dylan Rodríguez, and Sandy Enriquez have kept me afloat at the institution.

Lastly, thank you to the workers at Duke University Press—including Ryan Kendall, Olivia Schmitz, Chad Royal, and Lisa Lawley—for providing such invaluable guidance on and generous support for this project. From the moment I first met and spoke with her about the book project, Courtney Berger listened with attentive care, encouraging me to write in ways that remained true to the aims of the project. I am grateful for her gentle editorial guidance and her steadfast belief in the project.

May Palestine be free. May Korea be unified.

NOTES

AN END IS A RETURN TO THE BEGINNING

1 Million, "Felt Theory"; Lorde, "Uses of Anger"; Lorde, "Poetry Is Not a Luxury."
2 Lorde, "Poetry Is Not a Luxury," 37.
3 Since 2017, all US citizens have been banned from traveling to north Korea. The policy was implemented by the first Donald Trump administration (2016–20), was continued by the Joe Biden presidency (2020–24), and has been sustained by the second Trump administration (2024–present).
4 Here, I think of the critical scholarship of Jinah Kim, who describes insurgent melancholia as an agentive form of activism and organizing in the context of the Korean diaspora. Refer to Jinah Kim, "Insurgency of Mourning."
5 Sharpe, *Ordinary Notes*; Shimoda, *Afterlife Is Letting Go*.
6 I honor the feminist writers, scholars, and artists, including Audre Lorde, Gloria Anzaldúa, Elyse Semerdjian, Hazel Carby, Latipa, Theresa Hak Kyung Cha, and Clara Han, who underscore how the *personal* is a critical dimension of historical and theoretical writing.
7 S. Han, *Mu*, xiii.
8 For an especially incisive and compelling historical contextualization of han, refer to Sandra So Hee Chi Kim's "Korean 'Han' and the Postcolonial Afterlives of 'The Beauty of Sorrow.'"
9 As an example of this, I refer to statements made by Moon Jae-in, the president of South Korea from 2017 until 2022. While Moon was perceived as a supporter of Korean "comfort women's" struggle for justice against the Japanese government, he also expressed concern regarding the potential negative economic ramifications affixed to the "comfort women" issue. Following a January 2021 judgment handed down by the Seoul Central District Court—which ordered the Japanese government to pay damages to twelve former "comfort women"—Moon voiced concern about the financial fallout that could follow the ruling: "(Asset sales) will not be good for the relationship between South Korea and Japan" (quoted in Suzuki, "Moon 'Honestly Bewildered'"). Moon also added that com-

pensation had already been provided to survivors through the Reconciliation and Healing Foundation, established with ¥1 billion provided by the Japanese government. See Ji-eun Kim, "Moon Admits He Was 'A Bit Thrown.'"

THE EYE OF THE STORM

1 Didion, *Year of Magical Thinking*, 26.
2 Danticat, *Art of Death*.
3 My grandfather's name is phonetically spelled more often as Baek as opposed to Baik in English-language academic publications via the Revised Romanization System. Thank you so much to Ju Hui Judy Han and Jeongsu Shin for their translation support in regard to my paternal grandfather's publications and biographical information.
4 For an engaging study and exploration of the early historical roots of the Korean transnational adoption industry before 1950, refer to Pate, *From Orphan to Adoptee*.
5 As detailed later in this chapter, the 1953 armistice signed among combatants in the Korean War halted armed fighting without formally ending the war. Since then, no peace treaty has been signed, and the Korean Peninsula remains divided along the 38th parallel.
6 Clara Han's *Seeing Like a Child* discusses how the Korean War shapes everyday lives across multiple generations and diasporic spaces, less as hauntings or spectral ruptures and more as material living conditions.
7 In 2012, my twin sister, Cristiana Kyung-hye Baik, participated in what was then known as the Democratic People's Republic of Korea (or DPRK) Exposure and Education Program (or DEEP), organized by Nodutdol for Community Development, based in New York. Since 2017, the program has been suspended due to the travel ban placed on US citizens by Donald Trump's administration (2016–20, 2024–present) and extended by Joe Biden's administration.
8 As shared in the next chapter, the only person that I am aware of who migrated to the south with my maternal grandparents and their children was my grandfather's mother.
9 H. Kwon, *After the Korean War*, 100.
10 Joo Ok Kim, *Warring Genealogies*, 131.
11 Gallagher, "Thinnest Line."
12 It is ironic that most south Korean citizens are able to visit north Korea only if they relinquish their south Korean citizenship. In 2001, I relinquished my south Korean citizenship when I was twenty-one years old and became a US citizen.
13 Cristiana Kyung-hye Baik, "Wreckoning," in Baik, *Reencounters*, 162.

14 Jin-Hyouk Kim and Moon, "Socialist Camp's North Korean Medical Support"; Sonja Kim, "Missionaries."
15 The goddess of birth and fate in Korea is referred to as 삼신 할머니, or Grandmother Samshin (samshin also translates into English as "three grandmothers"). K. Kim, "Expanding the Role of Midwives."
16 In 1905, Korea became a protectorate of Japan via the Japan-Korea Treaty. In 1910, Korea was formally annexed and became a Japanese colony.
17 As Christine Hong insists, it is imperative to challenge the standard periodization of the Korean War—that is, with the war beginning in 1950 and ending in 1953—since the prolonged conflict has multiple beginning points and manifestations, including the Jeju 4.3. Uprising (a seven-year conflict that began in 1948 and ultimately took the lives of twenty-five thousand to thirty thousand people). Refer to C. Hong, "Introduction"; and Jongmin Kim, "Early Cold War Genocide."
18 Sohn, *Minor Salvage*, 29–31.
19 Kim Yunsik, *Paek Ch'ŏl munhak yŏn'gu*.
20 Initially, a list of forty-two pro-Japanese literary figures was jointly published on August 14, 2002, by the National Literature Writers' Association, the Institute for Research in Collaborationist Activities, the quarterly magazine *Practical Lecture*, the National Assembly Members' Association for Country and Culture, and the National Assembly Members' Association for Building National Spirit.
21 H. Kim, "Baek Cheol's Cultural Capital."
22 Email correspondence, June 22, 2009. To respect confidentiality, I have chosen not to disclose the name of this scholar.
23 While my paternal grandmother's family was from Suwŏn in southern Korea, my mother is convinced that my father's family resided in P'yŏngyang for some time, but I have been unable to confirm this.
24 These negative portrayals of the mother, stepmother, and mother-in-law are not unique or isolated to Korean popular culture but are endemic to other cultures as well, including US popular culture (for example, in films and television shows such as *Snow White*, *Crazy Rich Asians*, *Monster-in-Law*, and *Bewitched*—just to name a few). For critical articles regarding the shifting portrayals of Korean mothers and mothers-in-law in popular culture over time, refer to Oh, "*Mother's Grudge*"; Tilland, "Family Is Beautiful"; M. Kim, "Changing Relationships."

THE WIND PHONE

1 Sasaki's description of the wind phone is shared in *This American Life*, Episode 597, September 23, 2016, https://www.thisamericanlife.org/597/one-last-thing-before-i-go-2016.

2   Shimoda, *Afterlife Is Letting Go*, 253.
3   Sincerest gratitude and thanks to Jeongsu Shin for translating excerpts from Kim Yunsik's *Paek Chʻŏl munhak yŏn'gu* (A study of Baik Cheol). I am also grateful to Ju Hui Judy Han for translating segments from online biographies of my grandfather and for introducing me to Jeongsu.
4   Kim Yunsik, *Paek Chʻŏl munhak yŏn'gu*, 491. Translation by Jeongsu Shin.
5   Baek Cheol quoted by Kim Yunsik in *Paek Chʻŏl munhak yŏn'gu*, 495. Translation by Jeongsu Shin.
6   In English, this pen name translates to White Iron. I am uncertain why my grandfather used this name for his work.
7   "백철(白鐵) (Baekcheol)." In *Encyclopedia of Korean Culture*. Accessed September 15, 2023, https://encykorea.aks.ac.kr/Article/E0022415.
8   N. Kwon, *Intimate Empire*, 42.
9   Choe Je-u, *Chondogyo Scripture*, 50.
10 In the scripture translated by Kim Yong Choon and Yoon Suk San (the version cited in this book), *Chʻŏndogyo* is spelled as *Chondogyo*—without the diacritics commonly used in the McCune-Reischauer system.
11 M. Cho, "Chʻŏndogyoŭi 'munhwajuŭi'ka paekchʻŏl munhage michʻin yŏnghyang yŏn'gu" (A study of the influence of "culturalism" of Cheondogyo in the literature of Baek Cheol).
12 Choe Je-u, *Chondogyo Scripture*, 50.

A COOKING LESSON

1   V. Nguyen, "Interview."
2   For important work that addresses disability and chronic illness through a critical social justice lens, refer to Piepzna-Samarasinha, *Carework*; Page and Woodland, *Healing Justice Lineages*; Khúc, *dear elia*.
3   My twin sister, Cris, reminded me that while we were growing up, Mom would share cozy and colorful stories about her childhood days in Korea. But mostly, these stories were about her love for food, especially sweets and chocolate, at a time when her family lived in poverty and struggled to make ends meet. It wasn't until my mother was nearly in college that her family reaped the benefits of an investment her father had made a decade earlier in south Korea: Grandpa quietly purchased acres of land (fruit orchards, I am told) just north of Seoul, which he eventually sold for a very healthy profit in the mid- to late 1960s.
4   G. Cho, *Tastes Like War*, 7.
5   Janice Kim, "Pacific War and Working Women."
6   Young-Sun Kim, "Gendered Korean Colonial Modernity," 207.
7   Young-Sun Kim, "Gendered Korean Colonial Modernity," 207.
8   Janice Kim, "Pacific War and Working Women," 91.

9   Janice Kim, "Pacific War and Working Women," 92.
10 Janice Kim, "Pacific War and Working Women," 91, 87–88.
11 In her emergent research, Yumi Moon traces the histories of northern refugees to south Korea between 1945 and 1949. As Moon noted in her talk at the University of Michigan in January 2023, many of these refugees did not necessarily see themselves as counterrevolutionaries. Rather, they supported "the independence of their hometown" while playing key roles in shaping nationalism in Korea throughout the 1950s. Refer to "Nam Center Colloquium Series | Correspondence from the Soviet Zone: Northern Refugees and the Rise of Cold War Nationalism in South Korea, 1945–1949," Asian Languages and Cultures, University of Michigan.
12 H. Kwon, *After the Korean War*, 77.
13 H. Kwon, *After the Korean War*; S. Moon, *Militarized Modernity*.
14 H. Kwon, *After the Korean War*; N. Kim, *Memory, Reconciliation, and Reunions*.
15 N. Kim, *Memory, Reconciliation, and Reunions*, 7–8.
16 H. Kwon, *After the Korean War*, 68–71.
17 Troeung, *Landbridge*, 254. Troeung's book has been published in the United Kingdom, Canada, and the United States.
18 When I attempt to put into words the implications of family separation for Grandma's life, my mind veers to the experiences of other Korean women I've read about. In one example, historian Ji-Yeon Yuh refers to Grandmother Lee, who was separated from her three young children and husband while she served as a translator for the US military. The day after she crossed the 38th parallel with a military unit in June 1950, armed fighting erupted, and she was unable to cross the sealed border again. For the remainder of her life, the same dream haunted her nearly every night: Grandmother Lee stands in front of a black river, and her children are on the other side crying out for her. But an invisible force holds her down, and she cannot cross the bruising rush of water. She wakes up in a cold sweat. Grandmother Lee passed away without ever learning about her family's fate. Like so many other people separated from their families, her dreams were the only place where she was able to conjure her children's faces and hear their voices. Refer to Yuh, "Moved by War."
19 Recently, the US National Archives published, via its website, US Signal Corps films that document these journeys between 1950 and 1953. Refer to Behringer, "Korean War Refugees."
20 Sohn, *Minor Salvage*, 46–47.
21 When I inquired of my aunt why my grandfather wasn't immediately arrested or even killed by the military officer, she was uncertain and could not provide a definitive answer.
22 My aunties Kyung and Youngsuk were born in 1946 and 1949, respectively, in Seoul.

23 Lee, "Development of Photo Studios."
24 C. Han, *Seeing Like a Child*, 7.
25 E. Kim, *Curative Violence*.

THE DIASPORIC FAMILY ALBUM

1 Here, I refer to Thy Phu's rigorous engagement with diasporic family photographs within the Vietnamese diaspora. Refer to Phu, "Diasporic Vietnamese Family Photographs"; Phu, *Warring Visions*.
2 Campt, *Image Matters*, 7.
3 Hu, *Prehistory of the Cloud*.
4 Latipa, "Archives of Love."
5 Barthes, *Camera Lucida*.

GRIEF AND RETURN

1 I am grateful for the beautiful photography of Park Chanho, who documents the grief and mourning work of Korean shamans. Refer to Park Chanho, *Return*.
2 H. Kwon, *After the Korean War*, 105.
3 Heonik Kwon does not provide the name of Lee's wife in this account. *After the Korean War*, 105.
4 H. Kwon, *After the Korean War*, 36.
5 This aphorism is commonly attributed to the Sri Lankan intellectual, writer, and activist Ambalavaner Sivanandan. For studies that examine the critical linkages between imperialism, war, and the production of diasporas, refer to Sivanandan's *A Different Hunger* and *Race and Resistance*.
6 M. Nguyen, *Gift of Freedom*.
7 *Merriam-Webster Dictionary*, "return," accessed July 24, 2024, https://www.merriam-webster.com/dictionary/return.
8 Gina Kim, *Faces of Seoul*, 00:09:16.
9 Hobart and Kneese, "Radical Care," 2. In conversation with Hobart and Kneese's definition of radical care in white supremacist contexts, I also think of Ruth Wilson Gilmore's frequently cited definition of racism originally shared in her essay "Race and Globalization." For Gilmore, racism is "the state-sanctioned and/or legal production and exploitation of group-differentiated vulnerabilities to premature death, in distinct yet densely interconnected political geographies" (261).
10 Ruiz, "Light for a Light."
11 Ruiz, "Light for a Light," 456.
12 Ruiz, "Light for a Light," 456.

13 Ahmed, *Complaint!*
14 Seong Kim, "Lamentations of the Dead." For other books that address ancestral rites, as well as grieving and mourning practices and rituals in Korea and the Korean diaspora (especially in reference to Japanese colonialism, the Korean War, and neoliberal capitalism), refer to Horlyck and Pettid, *Death, Mourning*; S. Choi, *Right to Mourn*; and Kendall, *Shamans, Nostalgias*. Also refer to chapter 4 of my book *Reencounters*.
15 As I discuss in chapter 4 of my book *Reencounters: On the Korean War and Diasporic Memory Critique*, the violence that unfolded on Jeju Island during this period was not widely discussed by the south Korean public until the late 1980s and early 1990s. Even now, public descriptions of the horrifying violence—as an "incident," "massacre," or "uprising"—vary depending on the government in power in south Korea.
16 Different names are given to these ancestral cleansing rituals depending on the geographic location and historical moment. Refer to Pettid, "Shamanic Rites."
17 Herman, *Truth and Repair*, 3.
18 Espiritu and Duong, "Feminist Refugee Epistemology."
19 Espiritu and Duong, "Feminist Refugee Epistemology," 591.
20 Here, I think of the critical scholarship of David Eng and Anne Anlin Cheng, whose astute insights and writing first opened me to engaging with mourning and the melancholic within Asian American cultural contexts. I am also grateful for Ann Cvetkovich's and Lauren Berlant's work, who both reframe trauma—and, by extension, depression—in relation to the everyday and the agentive. Refer to Eng, *Racial Melancholia*; Cheng, *Melancholy of Race*; Cvetkovich, *Archive of Feelings*; and Berlant, *Cruel Optimism*.
21 Cacho, "Racialized Hauntings."
22 Cacho, "Racialized Hauntings," 41.
23 As I learned later, jesa is typically held the evening before a death anniversary, though I held this first ceremony on the day my father passed away.
24 CK, email to author, June 22, 2024.
25 Eunice Hyunhye Cho, email to author, June 2, 2024.
26 The bulk of this book's writing took place during the horrific and accelerated genocide of Palestinians in Gaza as well as the West Bank. Thus, I am especially grateful for a powerful statement published by Nodutdol (a grassroots Korean diasporic organization based in New York City) that clarifies the historical parallels and solidarities between Korea and Palestine. "Nodutdol Statement: Koreans for Palestinian Liberation," accessed October 23, 2023, https://nodutdol.org/koreans-for-palestinian-liberation/.
27 ENP, email correspondence with author, May 27, 2024.

28 Chang-Won Park, "Between God and Ancestors."
29 Chang-Won Park, "Between God and Ancestors," 260.
30 I am grateful for Don Mee Choi's brilliant body of poetic and visual work, which has impacted and informed my writing and scholarship in invaluable ways. See D. Choi, *Hardly War*; *DMZ Colony*; and *Mirror Nation*.

BIBLIOGRAPHY

Ahmed, Sara. *Complaint!* Duke University Press, 2021.
Baik, Crystal Mun-hye. *Reencounters: On the Korean War and Diasporic Memory Critique.* Temple University Press, 2019.
Barthes, Roland. *Camera Lucida: Reflections on Photography.* Hill and Wang, 2010.
Behringer, Ashley S. "Korean War Refugees in Signal Corps Films." *The Unwritten Record* (blog), National Archives, April 5, 2022. https://unwritten-record.blogs.archives.gov/2022/04/05/korean-war-refugees-in-signal-corps-films/.
Berlant, Lauren. *Cruel Optimism.* Duke University Press, 2011.
Cacho, Lisa Marie. "Racialized Hauntings of the Devalued Dead." In *Strange Affinities: The Gender and Sexual Politics of Comparative Racialization*, edited by Grace Kyungwon Hong and Roderick A. Ferguson. Duke University Press, 2011.
Campt, Tina. *Image Matters: Archive, Photography, and the African Diaspora in Europe.* Duke University Press, 2012.
Cheng, Anne Anlin. *The Melancholy of Race: Psychoanalysis, Assimilation, and Hidden Grief.* Oxford University Press, 2001.
Ch'inil Inmyŏng Sajŏn P'yŏnch'an Wiwŏnhoe and Minjok Munje Yŏn'guso (Committee for the Compilation of the Biographical Dictionary of Japanese Collaborators and the Center for Historical Truth and Justice). *Ch'in'il inmyŏng sajŏn* (*Encyclopedia of Pro-Japanese Figures*). Minjok munje yŏn'guso, 2009.
Cho, Grace. *Tastes Like War.* Feminist Press, 2021.
Cho, Miyoung. "Ch'ŏndogyoŭi 'munhwajuŭi'ka paekch'ŏl munhage mich'in yŏnghyang yŏn'gu" (A study on the influence of "culturalism" of Cheondogyo in the literature of Baek Cheol). *Inmunsahoe* (Journal of humanities and social sciences) 11, no. 2 (April 2020): 801–12.
Choe Je-u. *Chondogyo Scripture: Donggeyong daejon* (*Great Scripture of Eastern Learning*). Translated by Kim Yong Choon and Yoon Suk San with Central Headquarters of Chondogyo. University Press of America, 2007.
Choi, Don Mee. *DMZ Colony.* Wave Books, 2020.
Choi, Don Mee. *Hardly War.* Wave Books, 2016.
Choi, Don Mee. *Mirror Nation.* Wave Books, 2024.

Choi, Don Mee. *Translation Is a Mode=Translation Is an Anti-Neocolonial Mode*. Ugly Duckling, 2020.

Choi, Suhi. *Right to Mourn: Trauma, Empathy, and Korean War Memorials*. Oxford University Press, 2019.

Cvetkovich, Ann. *An Archive of Feelings: Trauma, Sexuality, and Lesbian Public Cultures*. Duke University Press, 2003.

Danticat, Edwidge. *The Art of Death: Writing the Final Story*. Graywolf, 2017.

Didion, Joan. *The Year of Magical Thinking*. Vintage, 2005.

Eng, David. *Racial Melancholia, Racial Disassociation: On the Social and Psychic Lives of Asian Americans*. Duke University Press, 2019.

Espiritu, Yến Lê, and Lan Duong. "Feminist Refugee Epistemology: Reading Displacement in Vietnamese and Syrian Refugee Art." *Signs* 43, no. 3 (Spring 2018): 587–615.

Gallagher, Beth. "The Thinnest Line: When Does a Refugee Stop Being a Refugee?" *University of Waterloo Magazine*, May 30, 2016. https://englishatwaterloo.wordpress.com/2016/05/30/the-thinnest-line-englishs-dr-vinh-nguyen/.

Gilmore, Ruth Wilson. "Race and Globalization." In *Geographies of Global Change*, Second Edition, edited by R. J. Johnston, Peter J. Taylor, and Michael Watts. Wiley-Blackwell, 2002.

Han, Clara. *Seeing Like a Child: Inheriting the Korean War*. Fordham University Press, 2020.

Han, Sora Y. *Mu, 49 Marks of Abolition*. Duke University Press, 2024.

Herman, Judith L. *Truth and Repair: How Trauma Survivors Envision Justice*. Basic Books, 2023.

Hobart, Hiʻilei Julia Kawehipuaakahaopulani, and Tamara Kneese. "Radical Care: Survival Strategies for Uncertain Times." *Social Text* 38, no. 1 (142) (March 2020): 1–16.

Hong, Christine. "Introduction: The Unending Korean War." *positions: asia critique* 23, no. 4 (2015): 597–617.

Horlyck, Charlotte, and Michael J. Pettid, eds. *Death, Mourning, and the Afterlife in Korea*. University of Hawaiʻi Press, 2014.

Hu, Tung-Hui. *A Prehistory of the Cloud*. MIT Press, 2016.

Kaisen, Jane, dir. *Community of Parting*. Self-distributed/Jane Jin Kaisen, 2019. 72 min., 13 sec.

Kendall, Laurel. *Shamans, Nostalgias, and the IMF: South Korean Popular Religion in Motion*. University of Hawaiʻi Press, 2009.

Khúc, Mimi. *dear elia: Letters from the Asian American Abyss*. Duke University Press, 2024.

Kim, Eunjong. *Curative Violence: Rehabilitating Disability, Gender, and Sexuality in Modern Korea*. Duke University Press, 2017.

Kim, Gina, dir. *Faces of Seoul*. Picture Book Movies, 2009. 93 min.

Kim Hye-won. "Paekchʻŏrŭi munhwajabonʾgwa sahoejabon—ʻabitʻusŭʾwa 'kubyŏljitki'wa 'silloedo'rŭl chungsimŭro" ("Baek Cheol's cultural capital and social capital—Focusing on 'habitus,' 'distinction' and 'trust'"). *Journal of Korean Language and Literature* 87 (2013): 283–312.

Kim, Janice C. H. "The Pacific War and Working Women in Late Colonial Korea." *Signs* 33, no. 1 (Autumn 2007): 81–103.

Kim, Jinah. "The Insurgency of Mourning: Sewol Across the Transpacific." *Amerasia Journal* 46, no. 1 (June 2020): 1–17.

Kim, Jin-Hyouk, and Mi-Ra Moon. "The Socialist Camp's North Korean Medical Support and Exchange (1945–1958): Between Learning from the Soviet Union and Independent Course." *Uisahak* 28, no. 1 (April 2019): 139–90.

Kim Ji-eun. "Moon Admits He Was 'A Bit Thrown' by Court Ruling on Comfort Women Issue.'" *Hankyoreh,* January 19, 2021. https://english.hani.co.kr/arti/english_edition/e_international/979474.html.

Kim Jongmin. "Early Cold War Genocide: The Jeju 4.3 Massacre and U.S. Responsibility." *Abusable Past (Radical History Review),* Forum 5.4, April 5, 2021. https://abusablepast.org/forum-5-4-early-cold-war-genocide-the-jeju-4-3-massacre-and-u-s-responsibility/.

Kim, Joo Ok. *Warring Genealogies: Race, Kinship, and the Korean War*. Temple University Press, 2022.

Kim Kyung Won. "Expanding the Role of Midwives in Korea." *Korean Journal of Women Health Nursing* 27, no. 3 (September 2021): 167–70.

Kim, Myung-Hye. "Changing Relationships Between Daughters-in-Law and Mothers-in-Law in Urban South Korea." *Anthropology Quarterly* 69, no. 4 (October 1996): 179–92.

Kim, Nan. *Memory, Reconciliation, and Reunions in South Korea: Crossing the Divide*. Lexington Books, 2017.

Kim, Sandra So Hee Chi Kim. "Korean 'Han' and the Postcolonial Afterlives of 'The Beauty of Sorrow.'" *Korean Studies* 41 (August 2017): 253–79.

Kim Seong Nae. "Lamentations of the Dead: The Historical Imagery of Violence of Cheju Island, South Korea." *Journal of Ritual Studies* 3, no. 2 (Summer 1989): 251–85.

Kim, Sonja M. "Missionaries and 'A Better Baby Movement' in Colonial Korea.'" In *Divine Domesticities: Christian Paradoxes in Asia and the Pacific,* edited by Hyaeweol Choi and Margaret Jolly. Australian National University Press, 2014.

Kim, Young-Sun. "Gendered Korean Colonial Modernity: 'Housewifization' of Korean Colonial Women and the Reconfiguration of Domestic Work." *Review of Korean Studies* 12, no. 4 (December 2009): 205–33.

Kim Yunsik. *Paek Chʻŏl munhak yŏn'gu* (A study of Baik Cheol). Yŏngnak, 2005.

Kwon, Heonik. *After the Korean War: An Intimate History*. Oxford University Press, 2020.

Kwon, Nayoung Aimee. *Intimate Empire: Collaboration and Colonial Modernity in Korea and Japan.* Duke University Press, 2015.

Latipa. "Archives of Love." *Nang Magazine*, no. 9 (2021): 54–68.

Lee, Kyungmin. "The Development of Photo Studios in Korea." Translated by Jeehey Kim. *Trans Asia Photography* 4, no. 2 (2014). http://hdl.handle.net/2027/spo.7977573.0004.203. Originally published in *Hwanghae Munhwa* (Hwanghae review) 51 (June 2006).

Lorde, Audre. "Poetry Is Not a Luxury." In *Sister Outsider: Essays and Speeches*. Crossing Press, 1984.

Lorde, Audre. "Uses of Anger." *Women's Studies Quarterly* 9, no. 3 (Fall 1981): 7–10.

Million, Dion. "Felt Theory: An Indigenous Feminist Approach to Affect and History." *Wicazo Sa Review* 24, no. 2 (Fall 2009): 53–76.

Moon, Seungsook. *Militarized Modernity and Gendered Citizenship in South Korea*. Duke University Press, 2005.

Moon, Yumi. "Correspondence from the Soviet Zone: Northern Refugees and the Rise of Cold War Nationalism in South Korea, 1945–1949." Lecture, Nam Center Colloquium Series, University of Michigan, Ann Arbor, January 25, 2023.

Nguyen, Mimi Thi. *The Gift of Freedom: War, Debt, and Other Refugee Passages*. Duke University Press, 2012.

Nguyen, Viet Thanh. *A Man of Two Faces: A Memoir, A History, A Memorial*. Grove Press, 2023.

Nguyen, Viet Thanh. "Interview: For Viet Thanh Nguyen, Writing Is an Act of Beauty and Justice." Interview by Eric Nguyen. *Electric Literature*, October 3, 2023. https://electricliterature.com/book-memoir-viet-thanh-nguyen-a-man-of-two-faces/.

Oh, Eunha. "*Mother's Grudge* and *Woman's Wail*: The Monster-Mother and Korean Horror Film." In *Korean Horror Cinema*, edited by Alison Peirse and Daniel Martin. Edinburgh University Press, 2013.

Page, Cara, and Erica Woodland, eds. *Healing Justice Lineages: Dreaming at the Crossroads of Liberation, Collective Care, and Safety*. North Atlantic Books, 2023.

Park, Chang-Won. "Between God and Ancestors: Ancestral Practices in Korean Protestantism." *International Journal for the Study of the Christian Church* 10, no. 4 (2010): 257–73.

Park Chanho. *Return: Korea's Rituals of Death, Spirits, and Ancestors*. Alpha Sisters, 2022.

Pate, Soojin. *From Orphan to Adoptee: US Empire and Genealogies of Korean Adoption*. University of Minnesota Press, 2014.

Pettid, Michael J. "Shamanic Rites for the Dead in Chosŏn Korea: Ancient to Contemporary Times." In *Death, Mourning, and the Afterlife in Korea: Ancient to Contemporary Times*, edited by Charlotte Horlyck and Michael J. Pettid. University of Hawai'i Press, 2014.

Phu, Thy. "Diasporic Vietnamese Family Photographs, Orphan Images, and the

Art of Collection." *Trans Asia Photography* 5, no. 1 (Fall 2014). http://hdl
.handle.net/2027/spo.7977573.0005.102.
Phu, Thy. *Warring Visions: Photography and Vietnam*. Duke University Press, 2022.
Piepzna-Samarasinha, Leah Lakshmi. *Carework: Dreaming Disability Justice*. Arsenal Pulp, 2018.
Ruiz, Sandra, "A Light for a Light: A Minoritarian Aesthetics and the Politics of Grief-Work." *Meridians: Feminism, Race, Transnationalism* 21, no. 2 (October 2022): 455–79.
Sharpe, Christina. *Ordinary Notes*. Farrar, Straus and Giroux, 2023.
Shimoda, Brandon. *The Afterlife Is Letting Go*. City Life Books, 2024.
Sivanandan, Ambalavaner. *A Different Hunger: Writings on Black Resistance*. Pluto Press, 1982.
Sivanandan, Ambalavaner. *Race and Resistance: The IRR Story*. Race Today Publications, March 1975.
Sohn, Stephen Hong. *Minor Salvage: The Korean War and Korean American Life Writings*. University of Michigan Press, 2022.
Suzuki, Takuya. "Moon 'Honestly Bewildered' by the Ruling in Favor of 'Comfort Women.'" *Asahi Shumbun*, January 18, 2021. https://www.asahi.com/ajw/articles/14116301.
Tilland, Bonnie. "Family Is Beautiful: The Affective Weight of Mothers-in-Law in Family Talk in South Korea." *Journal of Korean Studies* 21, no. 1 (March 2016): 213–44.
Troeung, Y-Dang. *Landbridge: Life in Fragments*. Penguin Random House UK, 2023.
Yuh, Ji-Yeon. "Moved by War: Migration, Diaspora, and the Korean War." *Journal of Asian American Studies* 8, no. 3 (October 2005): 277–92.

INDEX

Note: Page locators in *italics* refer to images.

abandonment, 134–35, 161–62
adoption. *See* transnational adoption
alcohol use, 16–19, 129. *See also* Baik, Inki
alienation. *See under* family
ancestors, 43, 47, 101, 120, 121–22, 127–29, 134–35; communication with, 46–63, 135–36, 149–50. *See also* posthumous translation; wind phone
archives: absences from, 7, 20–22; accessibility, 22, 107; family albums, 3, 23–24, 40, 86–88, 92, 100–110; found, 6, 22; images, *18*, *41*, *78*, *87*, *93*, *95*, *99*, *103*, *105*, *106*, *109*, *111*, *145*; memory, 8, 20, 79; official, 28–29, 107, 129, 173n19; preservation, 107–8. *See also* history
Archive's End, The. *See* Latipa

Baik, Coleen Eun-hye, 18–19, 29–30
Baik, Cristiana Kyung-hye, 29–30, 139, 150, 160
Baik, Inki, 15–45, 49, 58, 118–19, 125, 126–27, 151–55; as deviant subject, 137–40; images of, *42*, *145*, *163*; memories, 27–28, 36–37; relationship with father, 50–52, 54, 55, 61
Baik, Young Ok, 17–18, 75–77, 91–96, 133, 155; break from reality, 2, 70–72, 73–74, 93; depression, 70–71, 73–74, 77, 89, 92; images of, *69*, *93*, *95*, *99*, *163*
Baik Cheol, 3, 22, *23*, 35–37, 40–41, *41*, *42*, 46–48; as father, 49–50, 61; scholarship about, 35–37, 48, 49–50, 52–53, *53*, 60
Bari. *See* Kaisen, Jane Jin

Buddhism, 141–42, 149
bulgae, 9–10, *61*, 62–63, *96*, *116*, *146*

Campt, Tina, 99, 101
chilch'im. *See* Mu-ism
Ch'in'il inmyŏng sajŏn (*Encyclopedia of Pro-Japanese Figures*), 35, 171n20. *See also* Baik Cheol
Choi, Don Mee, 143, 148, 176n30
Choi Jeongsuk, 22–23, *23*, 33–35, 37–40, 57, 161
Ch'ŏndogyo, 58–61. *See also* Baik Cheol; Korea
colonialism: anticolonialism, 54; Japanese, 35–36, 53–56, 80–81, 127; US, 122–23, 127, 136, 153, 161; violence, 5–6, 8–9, 24–26, 54–58, 72, 81, 153. *See also* Ch'ŏndogyo
Community of Parting. *See* Kaisen, Jane Jin
complicity, 35–37, 53–55, 57; ch'inil, 55–56. *See also* Baik Cheol; colonialism
cooking, 68, *69*, 74–77, 90, 94. *See also* Baik, Young Ok
critical refugee studies. *See* feminist refugee epistemology

depression. *See* Baik, Young Ok; disability; illness
diaspora, 4, 24–26, 72, 77, 100–101, 135; diasporic family album, 101–13; diasporic family history, 46–47, 72, 77, 135. *See also* archives

diasporic grief, 3–7, 8, 28–29, 41–43, 72–74, 136–140, 160–62; communal, 125–27
Didion, Joan, 20
disability, 9, 74, 90–91. *See also* illness
disciplinarity, 4, 6, 7, 8
Duong, Lan. *See* feminist refugee epistemology

eclipse, 61–63. *See also* bulgae
embodiment, 3–4, 20. *See also* emotions; felt theory
emotions: ambivalence, 42–43, 107, 136–37; anger, 18–19, 83, 90; despair, 2; empathy, 135; expression of, 16, 77, 82, 136; forgiveness, 55, 138–39, 153–54; gratitude, 110, 122–23, 153; joy, 132, 133, 163; sadness, 76–77, 81, 83–84, 89; theorizing with, 3–4. *See also* felt theory
Encyclopedia of Pro-Japanese Figures. See *Ch'in'il inmyŏng sajŏn*; *see also* Baik Cheol
erasure poetry, 150
Espiritu, Yến L. *See* feminist refugee epistemology
ethics of memory, 72–73, 94

Faces of Seoul. See Kim, Gina
family, 5–6, 89; entanglement, 72–74, 75; estrangement, 2–3, 20–21, 23, 40–41, 47, 50–51; haunting, 47–48, 51–52, 62–63, 128, 161; history, 2–3, 7, 72–73, 76; patriarchs, 7, 79; separation, 5, 8–9, 32, 82–84, 173n18; silences, 7–8, 26, 39, 47, 79, 91, 101; partial silences, 28, 54, 73, 92
felt theory, 3–4, 6
feminist refugee epistemology, 131–32, 134
fire dogs. *See* bulgae

gajok, 83. *See also* family; hojŏk
gender, 9, 22, 39, 80–82, 85–89, 108, 142, 171n24; ideal womanhood, 7, 78, 80, 82,

89; nationalism, 90–91. *See also* working class; Korea
grief, 20, 120–23; writing with, 4, 42–43, 132
grief-work, 126, 132. *See also* diasporic grief; mourning

history; erasure, 6, 29, 127–28; unreliable narrator, 40
hojŏk, 25–26, 82. *See also* archives; Korea
Huh Bok Nam, 77–79, 80–89, 102, 108; images of, *78, 87, 99, 103, 109, 111*; sadness, 76, 77, 89

ilga, 83. *See* family
illness: chronic, 2, 89, 91, 92; communal, 9, 128–129; stigma, 74, 90; terminal, 2, 49, 84–85. *See also* alcohol use; Baik, Inki; Baik, Young Ok

jesa, 118–19, 121–22, 140–45. *See also* mourning; ritual

Kaisen, Jane Jin, 133–36, *137*, 138
Kim, Gina, 123–24
Kim Kiun, 77, 78–79, 91, *99*, 100, 111
Kim Saryang, 54
Kim, Sukyoon, 2, 100, 107, 112, *113*
kkut. *See* ritual
Korea, 4–5, 9, 24–26, 31–32, 53, 59; 4.3 Uprising, 127–28, 134–35, 175n15; "comfort women," 8–9, 81; han, 8–9, 90; immigration from, 5, 24–26, 56; Jeju Island, 31, 127, 171n17, 175n15; Korean Artists Proletarian Federation, 36, 53–54; Korean War, 26, 27, 29, 31–32, 83, 85–87, 121; New Woman, 80; P'yŏngyang, 29–30; Seoul, 88, 108, 124–25; Taedong, the, 30, 33–35; travel to, 21, 25, 28–30, 40, 123–24, 143; Women's Labor Volunteer Corps, 81
Koh Sunahn, 134–36, *137*. *See also* Kaisen, Jaine Jin

language, 22, 27, 52, 53, 54–55, 56
Latipa, 107–8
Lee, Dohee, 129–30, *130*, 131
Lorde, Audre, 3–4. *See also* emotions; felt theory

Man of Two Faces, A. See Nguyen, Viet Thanh
memory, 5, 47; erasure, 7–8; memory-gift, 33–35; sharing, 27–28, *28*, 75–76
memory keeper, 112, 119–20, 135
militarization, 24. *See also* Korea
Million, Dian, 3–4. *See also* emotions; felt theory
miyeok-guk, 68–70, 74. *See also* Baik, Young Ok
mothering, 76–77, 90
mourning, 120–23, 125–30, 133–35, 138, 143–45; shared, 131, 134, 135, 141–42. *See also* ritual
mudang. *See* Mu-ism; *see also* mourning
Mu-ism, 62, 127–29

New Woman. *See under* Korea
Nguyen, Mimi Thi, 123
Nguyen, Viet Thanh, 72
Nguyen, Vinh, 28–29
Nodutdol, 25, 29, 170n7, 175n26.

Palestine, 142, 163, 175n26
photographs, 101–2, 104, 107–8. *See also* archives
posthumous translation, 149–55. *See also* ancestors
power, 5–6, 107, 125–26. *See also* colonialism
preservation. *See* history

racial melancholia, 137
radical care. *See* mourning

reparative imaginaries: alternative lives, 7–8, 86–89; of ancestors' daily lives, 30, 33–35, 39–40, 50, 94; of displacement, 32, 101–2
return, 120, 123–25, 130, 150
ritual, 129–31, 134, 135–36, 142, 149–50; images of, *130, 148*
Ruiz, Sandra. *See* grief-work

Sasaki Itaru. *See* wind phone
silence(s), 52, 84. *See also under* family; violence
speculative history. *See* reparative imaginaries
speculative memory. *See* reparative imaginaries
ssitgim-gut. *See* Mu-ism
Still Quiet. See Thach, Trinh Mai

telomere time, 49. *See also* violence
temporality, 9–10, 20, 40, 49, 101–2, 140
Thach, Trinh Mai, 131–32
transnational adoption, 24, 135, 136

violence, 49, 126, 127; colonial (*see* colonialism); family, 8, 18–19, 51; silence as a response, 84
vision, 14, 15–16, 43

wind phone, 46–47, 160, 162. *See also* bulgae; grief; ancestors
Women's Labor Volunteer Corps. *See under* Korea
work, 15–18, 132, 138
working class, 39, 74, 78, 80, 85. *See also* gender
writing, 6, 7, 8, 58–59, 60–61; history, 29; letters, 46–63, *148*, 149–55, *156*; my, 16, 20–21, 26, *28*, *38*, 43, 93

INDEX · 185

CREDITS

Photographs of a solar eclipse (April 8, 2024) in chapters 1, 2, 3, and 5 are by Enji Chung. Reproduced with permission.

A film still from Jane Jin Kaisen's *Community of Parting* (2019) is included in chapter 5. Reproduced with permission.

An original photograph of Dohee Lee's performance piece *MU*/巫: *9 Goddesses* (photographer: Scott Tsuchitani, 2019) is included in chapter 5. Reproduced with permission.

www.ingramcontent.com/pod-product-compliance
Lightning Source LLC
Chambersburg PA
CBHW040515220526
45357CB00058B/1198